# AGAINST SOCIALISM

THE EDITORS OF NATIONAL REVIEW

Post Hill
PRESS

A POST HILL PRESS BOOK
ISBN: 978-1-64293-455-7
ISBN (eBook): 978-1-64293-456-4

Against Socialism


Cover art by Luba Kolomytseva



Post Hill Press
New York • Nashville
posthillpress.com

Published in the United States of America

# TABLE OF CONTENTS

## "In Defense of Markets" Special Issue

# INTRODUCTION

## BY RICH LOWRY

SOCIALISM is back. T. S. Eliot said that "there is no such thing as a Lost Cause, because there is no such thing as a Gained Cause." We thought our Gained Cause was having vanquished domestic socialism forevermore after the collapse of Soviet Communism in 1989. In the 1990s, Bill Clinton operated within the broad economic consensus established by Ronald Reagan, and when Republicans called Barack Obama a socialist, some on the left considered it a racially charged smear. But here we are: A self-avowed socialist nearly won the Democratic nomination in 2016 and is a serious contender this time. Another socialist, Alexandria Ocasio-Cortez, is the hottest thing in progressive politics today. The Green New Deal and Medicare for All are proposals for sweeping aggrandizements of government power on a scale not seen in this country since the New Deal, if ever. Meanwhile, some on the right are raising questions about free markets, or even rejecting them. If for nothing else, NR exists to stand up for important truths, even when they are embattled or out of favor. It is in that spirit that we publish this book, a twin special issue making the case for markets and against socialism.

If our cause wasn't nearly as gained as we thought two decades ago, it is incumbent on us to make the argument for it more vigorously than ever. Thanks for reading.

# SOCIALISM IS NOT DEMOCRATIC

## Nor is it compatible with the Constitution

**BY CHARLES C. W. COOKE**

Back in 2011, while covering Occupy Wall Street, I was accosted by a man wearing a large cardboard box. On this box, which he wore around his torso as might a child pretending to be a robot, he had scribbled down a theory that, at first glance, seemed more sophisticated than most that were on display. "Hey, *man*," he said to me, "it's up to *us*."

To explain, he turned around to reveal the other side of the box, which bore a single word: DEMOCRACY. Then, having paused for effect, he turned around again and pointed to the front, on which he had written down almost every single economic system that had been tried in human history: CAPITALISM, SOCIALISM, MERCANTILISM, AUTARKY, DISTRIBUTISM, FASCISM, FEUDALISM, POTLATCH, MUTUALISM, and so forth. "It's up to *us*," he said again. "It's *our* democracy, and we can choose the economy we want."

Further conversation revealed that he believed this quite literally. In his view, democracy was the sole nonnegotiable element of our political system, while everything else was up for grabs. If a majority wanted to nationalize the banks or abolish private property or bar all international trade or invade Brazil and harvest its resources, that was its prerogative. As might be expected, he had a prediction and a predilection: Socialism, he explained, was both the most likely system to be adopted, because it catered to the "majority, not the 1 percent," and the best, because it would fix all of America's problems without any downsides.

"It's up to *us*."

I have thought about this conversation frequently since then, because it highlights some of the core misconceptions held by socialism's champions, which are, in no particular order, that the retention of a democratic system of government makes massive state intervention more acceptable, that "capitalism" is a "system" in the same way as is "socialism," and that liberal democracy—and, in particular, America's brilliant constitutional order—can survive the establishment of a socialist economy. Because I was there to write about the protests rather than to get into prolonged arguments, I listened and probed rather than disputed his contention. Had I been debating him, however, my rejoinder would have been a simple one: No, it's not "up to us."

Or, at least, it's not up to "us" in the way that my friend in the cardboard box was using the word "us." As I write, ascendant elements within the American Left are engaged in a sustained attempt to reintroduce and rehabilitate the word "socialism," in part by prepending to it a word that has a much better reputation and an infinitely better historical record: "democratic." Voters should not be fooled by the rebranding, for there is no sense in which socialism can be made compatible with democracy as it is understood in the West. At worst, socialism eats democracy and is swiftly transmuted into tyranny and deprivation. At best—and I use that word loosely—socialism stamps out individual agency, places civil society into a straitjacket of uniform size, and turns representative government into a chimera. The U.S. Constitution may as a technical matter be silent on most economic questions, but it is crystal clear on the appropriate role of government. And the government that it permits is incompatible with, and insufficient to sustain, socialism.

This is deliberate. In the United States, and beyond, we do not think about our democracy in purely procedural terms. While majority rule on certain political questions is indeed deemed imperative, we nevertheless reject the notion that majorities may do whatever they wish, we demand that our institutions leave room for civil society and for individuals, and we insist upon a broad presumption of liberty that extends across all areas of human activity. It is reasonably well understood in this country that to place the word "democratic" in front of, say, "speech restrictions" or "warrantless searches" or "juryless criminal prosecutions" would be in no way to legitimize those things or to make them more compatible with the preservation of a free society.

It is less well understood that to place the word "democratic" in front of "socialism" is an equally fruitless endeavor—and for the same reasons. To those whose conception of "democracy" is limited entirely to the question of "Who won the most votes?" this may seem paradoxical. To those familiar with the precepts beneath the Anglo-American tradition, however, it should be quite obvious. Just as the individual right to free speech is widely comprehended as part of what we mean by "democracy" rather than as an unacceptable abridgment of majority rule, so the individual rights protected in property and by markets are necessary to the maintenance of a democratic order—in this, deeper, sense of the word. In the West, choosing to trade with a person in another country is, itself, a *democratic* act. Electing to start a company in your garage, with no need for another's imprimatur, is, itself, a *democratic* act. Banding together to establish a cooperative is, itself, a *democratic* act. Selecting the vendor from which you source your goods and services—and choosing what to buy from it—is, itself, a *democratic* act. Keeping the lion's share of the fruits of your labor is, itself, a *democratic* act. When governments step in with their bayonets and say "No!" they are, in effect, keeping your choices off the ballot.

Properly understood, the attempt to draw a hard line between "democracy" and "economics" is not only a fool's game but a game that socialists do not in fact play themselves. Ugo Okere, a self-described "democratic socialist" who ran for the Chicago City Council earlier this year, was recently praised in *Jacobin* magazine for explaining that "democratic socialism, to me, is about democratic control of every single facet of our life." That's one way of putting it, certainly. Another is "tyranny." Or, if you prefer, *democratic* tyranny. Alexis de Tocqueville observed that "the health of a democratic society may be measured by the quality of functions performed by private citizens." Lose those functions in America, and you lose democracy in America, too.

And then there is the question of socialism's substantive record, which is so extraordinarily disastrous that it renders my friend-in-the-box's theoretical argument useless even on its own terms. It is, in a strictly technical sense, "up to us" whether we choose to, say, smash ourselves repeatedly in the face with a hammer, but that is neither here nor there given that nobody in his right mind would elect to smash himself in the face with a hammer. We should avoid socialism with a similar diligence—and for similar reasons.

History has shown us that socialism exhibits three core defects from which it cannot escape and which its champions cannot avoid. The first is what Hayek termed "the knowledge problem." This holds that all economic actors make errors based on imperfect knowledge but that a decentralized economy will suffer less from this, partly because the decision-makers are closer to the information they need, and partly because each actor does not wield total control over everything but is only one part of a larger puzzle. The second problem is that, because socialism eliminates both private property and supply and demand, it eliminates rational incentives and, thereby, rational calculation. The third problem is that socialism, following Marx's dialectical theory of history, lends itself to a theory of inevitability or preordination that leaves no room for dissent, and that leads in consequence to the elevation of a political class that responds to failure by searching for wreckers and dissenters to punish. Worse still, because socialists view all questions, including moral questions, through a class lens, these searches tend to be deemed morally positive—bound, one day, to be regarded by History as Necessary. Together, these defects lead to misery, poverty, corruption, ignorance, authoritarianism, desperation, exodus, and death.

Ironically enough, they also lead to socialism's exhibiting a record of failure in precisely the areas where it is supposed to excel. Despite the promises in the brochure, socialism has been terrible at helping the poor; it has been terrible at helping women advance; it has been terrible for civil liberties; it been terrible at helping the environment; it has been terrible at attracting immigrants; it has been terrible at tolerating and protecting minorities; it has been terrible at fostering technology, architecture, and art; it has been terrible at producing agriculture; and, worst of all, it has been terrible at sharing power and resources—indeed, it has done precisely the opposite, creating new "ruling classes" that are far less adept, far less responsive, and far less responsible than the ones they replaced.

It has become something of a running joke that, whenever socialism's history is highlighted, its diehard advocates insist that "that wasn't *real* socialism." This defense is frustrating. But it is also instructive, in that it is an admission that, like perpetual motion, socialism has never been realized in the world. The U.S. Constitution has survived for so long because it was built upon the understanding that man is imperfect and always will be, because it accepts that selfishness is ineradicable and so must be harnessed, because it acknowledges that power corrupts as much in our era as it ever did, and because it makes provisions for the fact that disunity is inevitable in any free society. Capitalism, too, has survived because it is built on truth rather than myths. Socialism, by contrast, has failed each and every time it has been tried because it is predicated upon precisely the opposite—that is, precisely the *wrong*—assumptions.

One would have imagined that, at some point, "That wasn't real socialism . . ." would have been followed by ". . . and real socialism *can't* exist because man isn't perfectible, selfishness is ineradicable, power has needed restraining since the dawn of time, and political unity is a dangerous and undesirable myth." Alas, no such recognition has yet been forthcoming. In the 20th century, Communism killed at least 100 million people—by democide, by famine, by central planning, by war—and yet it is still acceptable to say in public that it was a "nice idea." In the post-war period, "democratic" socialism ravaged the economies of the West like a virus and required a counterrevolution to remove, and yet it remains sufficiently seductive to a slice of the public as to present a threat to the American order. Today, the states that have actively rejected socialism are growing fast (India, Poland, the former East Germany) while those that fell prey to the temptation are either moribund (Greece), tyrannies (China), or international pariahs (Cuba and North Korea)—and yet there is still a solipsistic cottage industry dedicated to blaming their successes and failures on decisions made by the United States. The damn thing is ineradicable.

And so we get Venezuela. That Hugo Chávez's centrally planned "Bolivarian Revolution" has descended into dictatorship, repression, starvation, and crisis was apparently genuinely shocking to a good number of the people who write about politics for a living. Six years ago, upon Chávez's death, the *Guardian*'s Simon Reid-Henry reflected the consensus view on the left by arguing that Chávez had shown "that the

West's ways aren't always best" by "[refashioning] Venezuelan democracy in ways that he thought better addressed the country's long-standing development issues." His paper's editorial board went one further, describing Chávez's work as an "unfinished revolution." Predictably enough, this was in fact a correct characterization of Venezuela's fate—just not in the way that the *Guardian* had anticipated. Five years after that edition went to print, Ricardo Hausmann, the former chief economist of the Inter-American Development Bank, was explaining that "Venezuela's economic catastrophe dwarfs any in the history of the U.S., Western Europe or the rest of Latin America."

Surprise!

"The West's ways aren't always best"? The Venezuelan president is now a ruthless dictator who has cracked down on free speech, prohibited mass political protests, and confiscated firearms from anyone who has been even remotely critical of him. Thirteen percent of the country's population has now fled, and those who have remained have been left so degraded by the government's price controls that they have gone years without toilet paper, meat, and other basic necessities and have in consequence taken to eating zoo animals for sustenance and to scouring garbage bags for supplies. According to the Pharmaceutical Federation of Venezuela, the country is suffering through an 85 percent medicine shortage and a 90 percent shortage of basic medical supplies. The child-mortality rate has increased 140 percent. Ninety percent of Venezuelans now live in poverty. This year, the IMF predicts, inflation will hit 10 million percent. All this in a country with the world's largest oil reserves—reserves greater than those of the United States by a factor of *ten*.

"It's up to *us*."

One of the great advantages to living at the tail end of 6,000 years or so of human civilization is the chance we have been afforded to look back and learn from the lessons accrued by others without having to go through the pain of learning them for ourselves. History is a complicated thing, and should be treated as such, but there are nevertheless a few core rules by which we can live: Do not inflict laws on others to which you would not subject yourself; ensure that you distribute power among several rival institutions, and, if possible, several geographical locations; never relinquish the right to free speech, the right to free conscience, the right to freedom of religion, the right to bear arms, or the right to a jury trial; insist on being represented by a parliament, and make sure that you prohibit that parliament from loaning its powers to a king, temporarily or permanently; do not ask people to give up more of their income than they are permitted to keep; and don't, whatever you do, be seduced by socialists bearing promises. And if you *are* seduced, get out before it's too late. You have nothing to lose but your chains.

# SOCIALISM AS EPIC TRAGEDY

## The idea millions killed and died for was a mirage

**BY JOSHUA MURAVCHIK**

THE saga of socialism constitutes an epic tragedy. It was the most popular political idea ever invented, arguably the most popular idea of any kind about how life should be lived or society organized. Only the great religions can compare. Within 150 years from the time the term "socialism" was coined, some 60 percent of the world's people were living under governments calling themselves socialist. Of course, not everyone who lived under such a regime shared its philosophy, but many millions did embrace socialism, join socialist parties, vote for socialist candidates, and even kill and die for socialism.

The powerful allure of socialism lay in its appeal to idealism. Every major religion affirmed the superior importance of the spiritual realm as compared with material things. Socialism spoke to this value system, promising a secular path to its fulfillment—and, even better, one that entailed little sacrifice. Socialists reasoned that if only property were owned in common, everything shared, and the fruits divided equally, people would no longer have cause to vie with one another.

A new day of brotherhood would dawn. Freed from competition and invidious distinctions, individuals could enjoy a closeness they had never known before.

And there was more. No longer obsessed with the scramble for wealth, individuals could instead pursue self-fulfillment. I might hunt in the morning, fish in the afternoon, and write criticism in the evening, said Marx. Individuals could thus focus on developing their talents. Every person, said Trotsky, could become a Beethoven or a Goethe.

There would no longer be want. Not only would the sharing of goods ensure sufficiency for all, but also, instead of wasteful production for profit, economies could be focused on producing for need. Schools and libraries might be built instead of casinos or brothels, mass transit or family sedans instead of thrill or prestige cars, and so on.

The early socialists, starting in the 1820s, created model communities, hoping to demonstrate the superiority of the system they espoused. These all fell apart, usually quickly. But the fact that the system proved difficult to put in place did not negate the beauty of the idea, and few socialists plumbed the question of why, exactly, it was so difficult to create and sustain this system.

In any event, Marx and Engels soon appeared and rescued hopes, dismissing the early experiments as "utopian" and thus devoid of meaning. Instead, the duo claimed to have discovered laws of history revealing socialism to be mankind's more or less inevitable destiny. The deus ex machina that would dig the grave of capitalism was the "proletariat," a fancy word for the working class. Ruthless competition would compel capitalists to squeeze the compensation of employees until the workers, finding themselves constantly more miserable and exploited, rose up and overthrew the system, replacing it with socialism.

Oddly, this prophecy did not induce complacency. On the contrary, Marx and Engels became intensely involved in socialist organizations and parties. In their footsteps, socialists thereafter balanced the confidence of being on the right side of history with political activism intended to help history along. But new disappointments were in store.

In the 1890s, half a century after Marx and Engels set forth this vision, their intellectual heir, Eduard Bernstein, the one who had been chosen by Engels to produce volume four of the socialist bible, *Capital*, just as he himself had produced volumes two and three from the notes Marx had left, confessed to the observation that events were not bearing out the Marxian prophecy. The workers exhibited no interest in revolution for the apparent reason that they had been experiencing steady improvement in their material conditions rather than the forecasted deterioration. Economic historians now estimate that the standard of living in the advanced countries roughly doubled over those 50 years. Bernstein had access to no such data, but in contrast to Marx and Engels, he hailed from the working class and was intimately familiar with its vicissitudes, and thus was well equipped to assess changes in diet, wardrobe, and the like.

Bernstein drew the logical conclusion. He abandoned socialism. He determined to continue struggling to wrest better conditions for the workers, but he said, "The 'final goal of socialism' is nothing to me." Others, however, were not ready to abandon the "final goal." Although workers' lives may have improved, their lot was still harsh. More important, the point of socialism was not only to ameliorate the plight of workers; the larger goal was to build a new society more harmonious and humane than any before.

In sum, socialism had reached a crossroads. If the workers were not going to create the revolution as predicted by the Marxian model, then a socialist had to choose. One could choose, as Bernstein did, to stick with the workers but give up on the revolution. Or one could choose to stick with the revolution but look to people other than the workers to bring it about. That was the choice of Lenin.

He shared Bernstein's premise. In his terminology, history had shown that, left to their own devices, the workers would achieve only "trade-union consciousness," not "revolutionary consciousness." In other words, they sought higher wages, not bloody upheaval. But Bernstein's conclusions enraged him. The majesty of socialism could not be forgone just because workers' standards of living had risen. If the workers would not make the revolution, someone else had to.

Lenin hit upon the idea of creating a party of professional revolutionaries who would fill this role. They would not merely act in the name of the workers or for the benefit of the workers. They would collectively constitute the "vanguard of the proletariat" even though Lenin acknowledged that individually they would not be, or would not mostly be, proletarians.

This metaphysical leap may have been hard to follow, but it worked—at least insofar as Lenin's band succeeded in seizing power and proclaiming the world's first socialist state. Knowing that he commanded the allegiance only of his "vanguard," an armed minority, Lenin then felt, with reason, that he had little means of ruling other than to prohibit opposition and cow the populace into obedience. He exhorted his followers to exert "merciless mass terror against kulaks, priests, and White Guards; persons of doubtful standing should be locked up in concentration camps."

Lenin, to be sure, harbored an extraordinary thirst for power, but he was not merely out for power. He had a mission: socialism. In Russia, where the economy was predominantly agricultural, that meant collective farming. But the farmers, wanting nothing of the sort, resisted passively. Faced with economic disaster and civil war, he backed down on collectivization. But his successor, Stalin, renewed the struggle, engineering a famine, in which some 5 to 10 million starved to death, in order to secure the peasantry's capitulation.

If Stalin was a tyrant of stupefying brutality—what previous despot had deliberately starved his own population?—he was matched or even outdone by such other Communist rulers as Mao and Pol Pot. Of this dynamic, Milovan Djilas, once a top leader of Yugoslav Communism, said: "How could they . . . act otherwise when they ha[d] been named by . . . history to establish the Kingdom of Heaven in this sinful world?" Had these men wished only to rule and enjoy the perquisites of unbridled power, they would have killed fewer. It was their devotion to an ideal that prompted them to slaughter millions of unresisting innocents.

Nor was this all. The idea propounded by Marxism of a redemptive future toward which history is trending but that can be helped along by mass violence proved open to permutation. Just as Lenin substituted the vanguard for the proletariat, Mao and Pol Pot added the wrinkle of substituting the peasants for the workers and then the vanguard for both. Mussolini, who was weaned on Marxism, spun another twist, replacing class with nation. He argued that downtrodden Italy belonged to the "proletariat" among nations while the wealthier states of northern Europe were the "bourgeoisie," the enemy. Then Hitler replaced the nation with the so-called Aryan race and identified the Jews as the enemy class of his National Socialism. Thus, the ideal of a new brotherhood yielded one episode of mass murder upon another, altogether sketching as sanguinary a chapter as history has ever known.

Of course, not all socialists followed the bloody trail Lenin blazed. Some, usually under the banner of parties calling themselves "labor" or "social democratic," insisted on pursuing only democratic and peaceful paths to the promised land of collective ownership and equal distribution. Over many decades they discovered, as Bernstein had foreseen, that these routes led no farther than the welfare state undergirded by a capitalist economy. The "socialism" that so many thought they could see over the horizon, that millions killed and died for, turned out to be a mirage. Its pursuit spelled one of history's saddest chapters.

# IF YOU WANT TO WANT . . .

## How socialism causes shortages

**BY JEFFREY TUCKER**

YOU can believe that socialism is wonderful, as apparently many people do, and no one will stop you. You will get plenty of support from the media and academic elite. You can rally around their Twitter handles, podcasts, and Kindle tomes.

On the other hand, the whole theoretical basis for the idea was completely smashed a century ago. From a historical perspective, every prediction that socialism would produce nothing but chaos, deprivation, poverty, suffering, and death turned out to be true. If both theory and history scream "Fail!"—and this failure affects things you claim to believe in, such as human rights and dignity—it might be time to rethink.

Among the most conspicuous of socialism's failings is its capacity to generate vast shortages of things essential for life. This is a universal feature of a socialist "economy," and it always has been. In Maoist China, there was no meat and no fat in which to cook anything, if you could find something to cook. In Bolshevik Russia, there were never enough cars, apartments, or even loaves of bread. Every Latin American socialist experiment produced the same. All of this was thoroughly documented in the 1997 treatise *The Black Book of Communism* (among thousands of other books).

And since that time, we have observed no serious change in Cuba: It's a life of scrounging around for basics, improvising repairs, and fear of falling buildings because materials necessary for repair are unavailable, with all technology stuck in time (pre-socialism).

In Venezuela, there is no meat, medicine, flour to make hosts for Communion, or reliable electricity, and the population is reduced to barter. The same is true in North Korea—where toilet paper is scarce and matches are housewarming gifts—the experience of which is a repeat of the tremendous deprivation of every other socialist experiment. Consistent with all evidence, "famine is a disproportionately prevalent outcome of socialist systems," writes American Enterprise Institute resident scholar Benjamin Zycher. There is no reason to think it will ever be otherwise.

There is a reason to think that many people will continue to deny that it matters. Consider the views of two London-based journalists, Alan Gignoux and Carolina Graterol, who were recently interviewed by *Counterpunch*. They looked at the absence of meat in Venezuela and praised the population for going vegetarian: "Mango trees are everywhere, so you can pick a mango whenever you want," Gignoux enthused. As for the energy shortage, Graterol said, "During blackouts, people told stories, played music, or went out and talked on the streets. It was a paradise, no TVs, smartphones, but real human contact."

Yes, they actually used the word "paradise" to describe Venezuela today. If certain leftists are unable to see why mass deprivation of food and energy is so bad, it seems hopeless that they will see cause and effect at work in small-scale instances of government intervention. After all, the entire economy doesn't need to be socialist to achieve the effect of shortage, restriction, and deprivation.

Microsocialism that disables market signals in any sector seems mostly to produce shortages, as price controls did for gasoline in the 1970s in the U.S., as rent control has done in New York City apartments, and as development restrictions have done in Silicon Valley. Too much regulation is another path to disabling market signals, and that also creates shortages, as it has in the U.S. child-care industry. The sector is so weighed down by regulation at all levels that it no longer benefits from the abundance-creating effects of market competition. And yet people are prone to blaming the free market for the consequences of these quasi-socialistic forms of intervention.

These results of shortage and deprivation under socialism are not random. There are explanations for them. With the rights to property denied and enterprise throttled through top-down control, the essential mechanisms that make economics work are radically disabled. It is also deeply demoralizing and demotivating to slave away in an economic structure that promises good for all but personally feels like a mandated rip-off. You can't quit your job, you can't find another, and you can't start something new. Your every association and decision is policed by someone who claims to know better.

If you look up what creates wealth, beautifully explained by Adam Smith, top-down coercion against person and property does not figure into the mix. But there is an even more fundamental problem, having to do with pricing. Socialism has never overcome it. It was first revealed in 1920, when Ludwig von Mises explained that rational economic planning would be impossible under socialism. Shortages are only the most conspicuous feature of a system that results in chaos and corruption.

The argument, which Kevin D. Williamson discusses at greater length elsewhere in this issue, is as follows.

Without the market forces of supply and demand (the trade that creates these forces; and private ownership of the means of production, which enables supply and demand to operate), all factories and industries will lose access to meaningful profit-and-loss accounting. Accounting signals relay information to owners about the success or failure of their enterprises. Without such accounting, there is no basis for managers of enterprises to make good decisions. You have no data on which to base your purchases, investments, production, hiring, wages, inventories, or anything else. You lose touch with the reality of the world around you. Such a system will be, quite literally, irrational and thereby subject to the whims of political elites.

This argument in 1920—precise, relentless, decisive, and seemingly unanswerable—came as a shock to European intellectuals. F. A. Hayek reports that Mises's point shook him from his own attachments to socialism.

What people didn't know at the time (communication was far more limited) was that Mises's proposition was already being proven in Russia. Three years earlier, to near-universal celebration among elite American intellectuals, the Bolsheviks had taken full control of Russia's government and had begun to implement their vision of socialism. Supply and demand, price signals, and private ownership were out. Lenin's first attempt to implement socialism came with full nationalization of industry, work mandates, controls on trade, pillaging of agricultural lands and produce, rationing and centralized distribution of everything, and a full ban on private enterprise.

This so-called War Communism was a comprehensive plan implemented with militarized ferocity. The results of this terror state were catastrophic. Production collapsed, falling by half. Money died and people were reduced to barter. Output for heavy industry fell to pre-revolutionary levels. The trains fell apart and stopped running. The grain harvest was half of what was needed to feed the population. And then there was famine that resulted in an estimated 3 to 10 million deaths between 1918 and 1921. That was the first comprehensive experiment in implementing socialism in a nation.

Protests and anger were palpable, and the Communist Party figured out it had a major political problem. In 1921, Vladimir Lenin reversed most of War Communism with his New Economic Policy, which permitted markets, ownership, trade, and profits. It was a temporary measure, but it saved the economy from total death, sparing millions of lives but also permitting the Communist Party to regain the control it was quickly losing. In time, the liberalization ended and the crackdowns began anew, leading to more suffering, shortage, deprivation, famine, and death.

That experience alone should have forever ended humanity's romance with socialism. For many socialists at the time, it was proof enough; one-time socialist Max Eastman, for instance, saw the wreckage firsthand and devoted the rest of his life to defending real freedom. But the disaster was blacked out by many media partisans of the experiment, so that most people in the West, even in Europe, knew nothing about any of it. It was many decades later when the news finally got out. But now we know, as the former socialist Robert Heilbroner admitted in *The New Yorker* in 1989, that "Mises was right."

So much for the purely theoretical explanation. In political reality, the ubiquity of shortage under socialism has an even more disturbing explanation. Economists Andrei Shleifer and Robert Vishny argued in a 1991 paper for the National Bureau of Economic Research that shortages under socialism serve the important purpose of providing bribe-based profits to the ruling class. That is to say, socialism's functioning, to the extent it functions at all, depends fundamentally on corruption—sneaking around the plan and gaming the system to survive.

The Shleifer-Vishny argument asserts that, because factories under socialism are considered public utilities, their managers cannot keep accounting profits because all profits (even fake ones) go to the state treasury. That result is bad both for the factory managers and for the ministries and bureaucracies that issue plans and prices. The only way for them to obtain personal benefit from the economic system is through bribes. Shortages increase bribe profits, just as surpluses reduce them. So the goal of every participant in the system is to restrict consumer availability as much as possible.

Over time, everyone learns to bribe, so corruption eventually displaces normal economic functioning. "The reason for pervasive shortages is self-interested behavior by ministry bureaucrats who set the plan prices and output," Shleifer and Vishny write. "These bureaucrats intentionally plan shortages in order to encourage bribes from rationed consumers." As unofficial transactions, the bribe profits can be privately held rather than being turned over to the treasury.

What's distinct about this argument is that it presumes that factory managers, workers, consumers, planners, and ministry officials—all part of a unified plan concocted by self-described socialists—are self-interested in the sense that they are seeking a better material life for themselves. This assumption is critical to their conclusions and contrary to most socialist theory, which presumes infinite benevolence at all levels of society, even to the point of the transformation of human nature itself. If you doubt that human nature can change, it is revealing to examine how socialism ends up working in real life.

Let's take a look at some history. The Shleifer-Vishny theory pertains particularly well to a fascinating period of Soviet history. After the Second World War and the death of Stalin, Nikita Khrushchev took over as Soviet leader, from 1953 to 1964. This is a period when the leadership genuinely believed that they could make socialism work to the point that it would produce more material prosperity than capitalism did in the West. (This is what Khrushchev meant when he promised "We will bury you.") With full input from

Soviet economists, all of them well trained, they tried desperately to cobble together a system of planning that made rational sense without relying on "bourgeois" market forces.

It was an enormous failure. With Stalinism at an end, so too was the mass terror. But with the new Khrushchevian stability came the entrenchment and ubiquity of the bribe economy, the petty corruption of everyday life, and the spreading of a gritty mass cynicism. Khrushchev was never able to make socialism work, and he spent his last years as a discredited, dejected, and sad old man on a park bench. He became a non-person. "In his activities, there were elements of subjectivism and voluntarism," reads the only mention of him in the *Great Soviet Encyclopedia*. (I wish everyone could read *Red Plenty*, by Francis Spufford, an accurate historical account of the Khrushchev years put in novel form, to understand why even non-terroristic versions of socialism are doomed to fail.)

For only so many decades can you believe that cracking down on corruption will fix a system that fundamentally depends on that very thing. Eventually, the Soviet system died of exhaustion, revealing an economy thrown back in time, universal cheating and cynicism, a dilapidated capital infrastructure, low-quality everything, and shortages of consumer goods that the poorest people in the West take for granted. Thus ended a 70-year attempt to implement socialism.

And what about the theory that the only real alternative to market signaling and free enterprise is the bribe-based intentional shortage? It has an intuitive plausibility. We can see how this works even in developed economies. After all, a government can disable price mechanisms and institute a bribe economy without full-on socialism. When it does, what you find is evidence of institutionalized shortages.

The taxi industry in New York, a municipal monopoly without competitive pressure, worked for decades to create a shortage of services, and then ride-sharing shattered that model. Every industry that requires occupational licensing—from lawyering to hair braiding to flower arranging—is working to restrict supply in order to drive up prices. And one likely reason that Congress declines to adopt a flat tax is that it would end the gray market of lobbying for favors in the tax code; offer hard-to-get tax breaks and you drive up the price of exemptions and therefore the private benefit to those in power.

What history and theory show about socialism is that in real life it has nothing to do with social welfare, improved conditions for humankind, or justice, much less fine-tuning the global climate to make it perfectly match scientific prognostications. Even when it doesn't achieve economic collapse and famine, socialism defaults to an economy of restriction and corruption and the granting of terrible power to the ruling class, which then uses the system to pillage what it can while the masses suffer.

Now, I'm very aware of the tendency to write off all theory and history with the usual protest: This is not the kind of socialism *I* favor, because I'm a *democratic* socialist! You can add any adjective you want (from "syndicalist" to "nationalist"), but the effects of disabling prices, collectivizing property, suppressing market signals, and empowering ministries of control will always be the same. Economic reality doesn't care about your visionary politics.

Socialism in real life results in precisely the caricature of capitalism that socialists themselves have denounced for centuries—and in the economic chaos and impoverishment that Mises predicted and explained in 1920. If you love deprivation, constriction, and general limits on material aspirations, plus a tyrannical ruling class that oppresses everyone else, you will love what socialism can and does achieve. Indeed, misery seems to be its only contribution to economic history.

# THE IGNORANCE THAT KILLS

## Central planners never know enough, and mayhem tends to follow

**BY KEVIN D. WILLIAMSON**

IN his 1920 paper "Economic Calculation in the Socialist Commonwealth," the economist Ludwig von Mises dealt what should have been an intellectual death blow to socialism, showing, as he put it, that "rational economic activity is impossible in a socialist commonwealth." Mises expanded on the argument in his *Socialism*, and F. A. Hayek took up what came to be known as the "knowledge problem." Socialism, which purported to be scientific before it purported to be humanitarian (both claims have proved false), assumes that all relevant knowledge is essentially scientific in character and that economic problems may be solved in more or less the same way as engineering problems.

But there are other kinds of knowledge—local, temporary, transitory, dependent, subjective, situated in complex nests of subordinate and superordinate relationships. In Hayek's view, it is this knowledge that guides the "constant small changes which make up the whole economic picture."

There is beyond question a body of very important but unorganized knowledge which cannot possibly be called scientific in the sense of knowledge of general rules: the knowledge of the particular circumstances of time and place. It is with respect to this that practically every individual has some advantage over all others because he possesses unique information of which beneficial use might be made, but of which use can be made only if the decisions depending on it are left to him or are made with his active coöperation. We need to remember only how much we have to learn in any occupation after we have completed our theoretical training, how big a part of our working life we spend learning particular jobs, and how valuable an asset in all walks of life is knowledge of people, of local conditions, and of special circumstances. To know of and put to use a machine not fully employed, or somebody's skill which could be better utilized, or to be aware of a surplus stock which can be drawn upon during an interruption of supplies, is socially quite as useful as the knowledge of better alternative techniques. And the shipper who earns his living from using otherwise empty or half-filled journeys of tramp-steamers, or the estate agent whose whole knowledge is almost exclusively one of temporary opportunities, or the arbitrageur who gains from local differences of commodity prices, are all performing eminently useful functions based on special knowledge of circumstances of the fleeting moment not known to others.

The socialists of Hayek's and Mises's time believed that a properly empowered bureaucracy overseen by a committee of disinterested experts could comprehend the entirety of an economy—within an industry, within a country, or around the whole globe—given sufficient resources and scope of action. This was rooted in what was contemporary scientific thinking. In 1814, around the same time that Charles Fourier was writing his utopian socialist blueprint *The Social Destiny of Man*, Pierre-Simon Laplace published *A Philosophical Essay on Probabilities*, in which he posited what came to be known as "Laplace's Demon," which he described as "an intellect which at a certain moment would know all forces that set nature in motion, and all positions of all items of which nature is composed." In Laplace's thought experiment, "if this intellect were also vast enough to submit these data to analysis, it would embrace in a single formula the movements of the greatest bodies of the universe and those of the tiniest atom; for such an intellect nothing would be uncertain and the future just like the past would be present before its eyes." This is the idea of scientific determinism, which holds that if one could know the exact location and momentum of every atom in the universe (Werner Heisenberg had not yet thrown in the monkey wrench of uncertainty), then the future of the universe and everything in it could, in theory, be calculated according to the laws of physics.

The socialists themselves were quite taken with the idea, hence the strange history of "Soviet cybernetics," by means of which the central planners in Moscow imagined that they might develop a computer system so powerful that it could consider every variable in society at once and spit out scientific maxims about how many acres of potatoes to plant, and when and where to plant them. The prestige of science in the middle of the 20th century was enormous, and such dramatic scientific advances were being made so regularly—in the Soviet Union as elsewhere—that this did not seem entirely implausible.

It is precisely this view that Hayek is responding to:

> *If* we possess all the relevant information, *if* we can start out from a given system of preferences, and *if* we command complete knowledge of available means, the problem which remains is purely one of logic. That is, the answer to the question of what is the best use of the available means is implicit in our assumptions.

Mises and Hayek intuited (and showed) that complete knowledge was not attainable in social, economic, or political questions. Later, scientific studies of chaos and complexity worked out that in many cases of complex adaptive systems—such as markets and evolution—knowledge of the sort Laplace imagined is not available even in principle. In *Complexity: A Guided Tour*, computer scientist Melanie Mitchell of the Santa Fe Institute writes that "two major discoveries of the twentieth century showed that Laplace's dream of complete prediction is not possible, even in principle." The first was Heisenberg's "uncertainty principle," but that applies only at the quantum level, "an interesting curiosity, but not one that would have much implication for prediction at a larger scale—predicting the weather, say. It was the understanding of chaos that eventually laid to rest the hope of perfect prediction of all complex systems, quantum or otherwise." In chaotic systems—Mitchell lists "cardiac disorders, turbulence in fluids, electronic circuits, dripping faucets" as examples—seemingly trivial uncertainties in measurement can produce staggering errors in predictive models. Chaos is the reason we cannot accurately predict the formation and behavior of hurricanes, even though we know a great deal about them and have a great deal of data to work with. Economies are even more difficult to predict and to manage, because market participants will react in unpredictable ways to intervention.

It is a little ironic that Hayek spent so much of his career warning against the scientific pretenses of economics and his profession's mathematical manias only to see his work incorporated into a broad scientific theory expressed in recondite equations.

Some of the intellectual socialists of the 20th century took this criticism seriously and responded seriously if unsatisfactorily, inventing such ultimately incoherent ideas as "market socialism." And they have largely abandoned their plans for unitary central planning of entire national economies, turning instead to trial-and-error approaches to managing markets (e.g., the Affordable Care Act) and to limited, industry-specific management schemes—as though central planning on the installment plan were any more rational than the whole-enchilada version.

If this sounds a little esoteric, there are some well-understood, down-to-earth applications. Compare the U.S. food-stamp program with socialist management of agriculture, whether through collective farming or by other means.

The food-stamp program has its defects, to be sure: There is fraud, and abuse, and malingering, and food stamps create some poor economic incentives. But, generally, the program does what we want it to do: It helps some very poor people to get more and better food. Food stamps are welfare, not socialism. Socialism—central planning—would be something more like the government's trying to direct not only the farms but also the food-distribution networks, the grocery stores, and, inevitably, household diets and food economies. Even in their least ambitious forms (e.g., in Venezuela), those kinds of socialist undertakings have proved catastrophic. For all the gulags, purges, and massacres, the major socialist powers of the 20th century killed far more people through starvation than with bullets, sometimes intentionally (the Holodomor in Ukraine), sometimes through pure mismanagement, and sometimes a bit of both. For American conservatives, the conclusions are obvious when it comes to things such as K–12 education, which is one of the few truly socialized enterprises in the United States and, not coincidentally, one of the most defective. The conservative preference for the voucherization of social services is the Right's intelligent response to the problems of central planning, but it is by no means an intrinsically right-wing position. It is simply an acceptance of the fact that having taxpayers pay for welfare services is a different and more manageable thing than having government act as a direct provider of welfare services. No modern state outside of libertarian fantasy restricts itself to the provision of public goods (goods such that your consumption does not prevent my consumption and neither of us can be forced to pay for our consumption—e.g., the light of a lighthouse).

But the more intelligent governments have largely given up on central planning, even at the single-industry level. The Nordic social democracies so dear to the self-styled socialists of the United States mostly have been divesting themselves of state enterprises; indeed, the most common kind of socialism remaining in the world today is the one least loved by Bernie Sanders et al.: the oil company, many of which remain state-run. Even many reasonably successful state-run enterprises, such as the Swiss railroads, have been converted into stock corporations or reformed in other market-oriented ways.

For a too-brief period at the turn of the century, most mainstream progressives and conservatives were in broad agreement about some substantial part of the mechanics of welfare, including the desirability of letting markets work where possible. There was disagreement about how much to spend, about eligibility, about work requirements for welfare, and the like, but the central-planning impulse seemed to have crumbled with the Berlin Wall. But the "fatal conceit," as Hayek called it, is immortal.

The anti-capitalist Right flirts with it from time to time, too—for instance, in Republican presidents' desultory forays into the steel industry or the question of where the components of catalytic converters for automobiles are assembled, not normally matters about which one would consult a hotelier. The Wilsonian instinct for "war socialism" occasionally affects Republicans, usually abetted by pork-barrel politics. That is why we have a national "strategic helium reserve," and many other silly things.

The subtitle of Hayek's *Fatal Conceit* is "The Errors of Socialism." Of course Senator Sanders and Representative

Ocasio-Cortez have failed to learn from those errors, in the same way that they have failed to learn from anything. You cannot call yourself the party of science and the party of socialism, too. You have to choose one or the other.

# OF SOCIALISM AND HUMAN NATURE

## Why the ideology fails—and succeeds

**BY JOHN O'SULLIVAN**

One of Margaret Thatcher's more quoted sayings is "The facts of life are conservative." It's a remark that covers a great deal of ground, since it applies to entire societies as well as to individuals. In conventional politics it applies most obviously to economic policy. There the facts of life teach that you can't spend more than you earn, at least in the long run, and that if you borrow to finance an investment that pays less than the interest on your loan, you'll end up eventually in Carey Street (where the bankruptcy court is located). In work and personal life, they recommend diligence, sobriety, service, loyalty, fidelity, gratitude, and respectability. Victorian middle-class reformers, who succeeded in transforming boisterous, drunken, rowdy, criminal, and sexually promiscuous slum dwellers into model citizens and parents, did so in part by formulating these facts of life as moralistic epigrams that schoolchildren were required to copy down in the course of learning to write legibly. Thus, we got gems such as "The man who watches the clock will always be one of the hands" and other, more solemn instructions.

Hence the title of perhaps the most famous work by Rudyard Kipling, a poet greatly admired by Thatcher: "The Gods of the Copybook Headings." The Gods in question are the facts of life formulated as rules of virtuous and prudent behavior. As Kipling mordantly observes, these rules are much mocked by those who see them as obstacles blocking shortcuts to the "Fuller Life," but the consequences of ignoring or defying them can be terrible: "But they always caught up with our progress, and presently word would come / That a tribe had been wiped off its icefield, or the lights had gone out in Rome."

Yet, as Kipling's poem records, throughout human history, in one way or another, men and women have been persuaded to go down the road to perdition by glittering promises of a fuller life and a better world. He shows too how dire consequences followed from the hubristic self-confidence of the "smooth-tongued wizards" who offered these visions. On national security, for instance:

> When the Cambrian measures were forming, They
>     promised perpetual peace.
> They swore, if we gave them our weapons, that the
>     wars of the tribes would cease.
> But when we disarmed They sold us and delivered us
>     bound to our foe,
> And the Gods of the Copybook Headings said: "Stick
>     to the Devil you know."

Or on religion and family policy:

> On the first Feminian Sandstones we were promised
> the Fuller Life
> (Which started by loving our neighbour and ended
> by loving his wife)
> Till our women had no more children and the men
> lost reason and faith,
> And the Gods of the Copybook Headings said: "The
> Wages of Sin is Death."

Kipling was writing in 1919, at the dawn of the age of socialism, after the carnage and moral chaos of the Great War (in which his son had been killed), and just as Soviet Communism was winning in Russia and, as it then seemed, in much of Europe as well. His personal tragedy and the collapse of the European order before the barbarism of the Left seemingly combined to give him a piercing vision of the worse things that were to come from that direction. It's decidedly eerie how he repeatedly foresaw the progress from folly and idealism to shame and defeat in different areas of life and policy before a single socialist (or fascist) government was sufficiently established to set about implementing its ideology.

Three distinctions must now be drawn, however. First, the facts of life are not the same as the facts of human nature in the above sketch. If they were the same thing, we would learn from our mistakes rather than endlessly repeat them. Human nature persuades us to ignore the risks of foolish or utopian proposals; it also incentivizes us to exploit or evade the ugly consequences of their implementation. Human nature is the set of hopes, ambitions, and ideals that explains why socialism succeeds politically, but also the hopes, ambitions, and ideals that explain why socialism eventually fails economically, socially, morally, and thus politically too.

The second distinction is that our virtues are implicated in the rise and fall of socialism almost as much as our vices. That's why I used the phrase "glittering promises of a fuller life *and a better world*" a few paragraphs earlier and twinned "folly and *idealism*" in the previous one. Socialism is a powerful temptation to commit the worst of crimes precisely because it also appeals to our compassion and desire for social improvement. It gives us a strong excuse to impose our will on others unlawfully and even murderously.

And the third distinction is that among political philosophies, both conservatism and liberalism are also vulnerable to folly and wickedness—but to a lesser extent than socialism. It's easy to see why. Conservatism is a set of ideas about restraint, caution, and prudence. Its liberty is an *ordered* liberty. It distrusts government programs, social experiments, and utopianism on principle. Liberalism shares some of these concerns. Its preference for minimal government also limits its potential for state oppression. But liberalism's desire to demystify and replace traditional society with "rational" political structures and freely chosen social relations means that it blunders smilingly into revolutions under the optimistic banner of Reform. In practice, liberalism divides into economic liberals, who drift into conservatism for prudential reasons, and social liberals, who cannot resist the radical appeal of socialism but usually end up regulating popular social attitudes rather than industries. The risks attendant upon socialism are far greater, or at least more visible from the start. As the doctrine that the purpose of the state is to reform society along lines of social justice, it invites far greater social conflict. Even if there were enough justice to go around—which there isn't—that task would still require formidable state coercion to reorder property and other rights to benefit the proletariat or favored groups while depriving others of their common legal rights. And with every "socially just" expropriation, there would come more resistance, and in response to that resistance, more state coercion, and in response to that, the disruption of economic relations . . . and so on ad infinitum.

For the last time, let's hear from Kipling, on this very highly topical topic:

> In the Carboniferous Epoch we were promised abundance for all,
> By robbing selected Peter to pay for collective Paul;
> But, though we had plenty of money, there was nothing our money could buy,
> And the Gods of the Copybook Headings said: "If you don't work you die."

Under socialism, moreover, working is not enough. As Trotsky helpfully pointed out, you also have to conform. And obey. And applaud. And sometimes you die anyway. Some socialists in the Soviet Union were killed while still applauding.

Others writing in this special issue of *National Review*, notably Joshua Muravchik and Jeffrey Tucker, deal more than effectively with some of the technical reasons for the rise and failure of socialism. "Practical men" and some social visionaries, such as H. G. Wells, supported the planned economy of socialism because they imagined it would be less wasteful than market competition. In practice, of course, economic planning disrupted the price signals that the free market uses to ensure that industries produce goods that people want rather than those the planners think necessary. When that happened, the stores were full of unwanted surplus products alongside empty shelves and long queues of frustrated consumers. Planning produced some goods nobody wanted at any price: Khrushchev once complained that a factory, meeting the requirements of a quota expressed in quantitative terms, manufactured chandeliers so large and heavy that they pulled down the ceilings wherever they were installed. And, in the end, "really existing socialism" turned the whole of the Soviet Union and Eastern Europe into one vast economic wasteland.

But I'm more interested here in the attitudes that fueled the rise and decline of socialism—and usually ended in their own frustration. For many different sides of human nature conspired to support the socialist transformation of society. Some were transparently objectionable vices—for instance, envy.

If greed is supposedly the characteristic capitalist vice, envy is the typical socialist one. Envy, indeed, has most of the unpleasant consequences of capitalism—it is socially divisive, productive of conflict, encouraging of hostility towards those envied, and discouraging of everyone else's improving their lives and status—without the saving grace of greed, which leads to work, saving, and investment. Compare the relative damage to society caused by the crimes of socialism and capitalism. Both impoverish their victims, but crimes of envy can kill them too and spread a disabling fear throughout society. As Madsen Pirie of the Adam Smith Institute in London once asked: "When was the last time you were afraid to go out at night in case you were embezzled?"

Another was the power worship, allied to envy, of the intelligentsia. Literary critics, failed politicians, provincial academics, "pure" scientists, and unemployed artists all thought that they could run society and industry more competently and more generously than the capitalists and managers who were actually doing so. Marxism had given them the key. But Marxism is a fraudulent intellectual-labor-saving device that gives its converts the illusion that they can understand and solve any social problem without needing to learn much about it. The template will explain it to them. Its doctrine that ownership of the means of production defined social class, for instance, meant that it first missed and then resisted the advent of the managerial class and its rise to dominance. As a result, it creates a kind of lumpenintelligentsia that, while seeking to enforce Marxist dogma on everything from agriculture to musicology, gets in the way of everything from economic efficiency to the pursuit of scientific truth. Those who object find themselves sidelined at best, executed at worst—and the Soviet peoples got years of Lysenkoism and failed crops.

It is the social virtues, however, that have the most contradictory relationship with socialism. This was seen in 1970s social-democratic Britain as well as in harder socialist regimes. Good people in free societies are inspired to support socialism because they want to lift up the poor, help younger people to be less materialistic, and free themselves from their own guilt at what they feel is undeserved prosperity. The first two motives are decently honorable, but they don't necessarily lead to better outcomes for their supposed beneficiaries. The third motive is usually mistaken and, when persisted in, actually neurotic. Besides, the motives of aid givers are less important than whether the giving benefits those receiving it.

Still, let's consider each motive in turn.

First, charity. Lifting up the poor from poverty is an unalloyed good if it ends with their being self-reliant. Even if it achieves that aim only partially, it's still better than doing nothing. If, however, it reduces an independent but poor working man to a pauper who lapses into apathetic dependency, it has done more harm than good. Much thought over two centuries has been devoted to designing anti-poverty programs that help the poor towards self-reliance. Modern socialists, unlike the early working-class "ethical socialists," tend to disapprove of placing conditions on aid to the poor ("workfare"), usually instead viewing receipt of the aid as an unqualified right. That sounds generous. But not only does it trap the poor in long-term dependency, it also undermines what the Anglo-American scholar Shirley Letwin called the "vigorous virtues" among their neighbors.

Governments occasionally use focus groups to judge the practicality or success of their policies. One such focus group in Britain in the 1980s included a young couple who proudly told how they had saved enough money to apply for a mortgage and buy a house. They were made to look and feel foolish a moment later when their sharper neighbors advised them on how to game the system to get a home more cheaply from the government. When socialists start a program to lift the poor out of poverty, they end up trapping them in it. The final stage of this collectivist version of the rake's progress is for the more sophisticated members of the lumpenintelligentsia to condemn the virtues of self-reliance and hard work as a shameful individualist strategy that betrays the socialist collective—or, in an American racial context, as "acting white."

Much the same is true of apparently high-minded defenses of socialism, often coming from Christian leaders, as a system that is morally superior to materialistic and selfish capitalism. In reality, the scarcity of everyday goods in a socialist economy makes people even more materialistic than they are in the logo-obsessed West. Corruption flourishes to meet demands that socialism denies. In the later stages of Soviet Communism, a woman would sell herself for a pair of jeans; in Venezuela today, people exchange family heirlooms for a little food. But there are always hard-currency stores for socialist elites—and more than that for Politburo members. When I asked a Mont Pelerin guest in 1974 about his day job, he replied that I must understand why he could give me only the sketchiest account: "I manage the private hard-currency accounts of Soviet leaders in the West."

Such contradictions and hypocrisies are hidden only from those who don't wish to know about them. When their existence becomes undeniable, most comfortably-off foreign admirers of socialist regimes condemn them only formally and then carry on as before. Their admiration for leftist despotisms is really a roundabout neurotic rejection of their own societies and as such not to be taken seriously. It's the political equivalent of a society hostess's dressing like a dominatrix: It's intended to show contempt for dull middle-class virtues.

Hard-core progressives are a different matter. They are serious revolutionaries and either invent contorted justifications for socialist scandals—virtues are transformed by theory into vices and vices into virtues—or simply deny the plain evidence of their own senses: As each socialist paradise is shown to be a kleptocratic hellhole, the caravan of Sandalistas simply moves on to the next one without apology.

They make a trivial and contemptible contrast to those who in the late 19th and early 20th centuries sensed and predicted the paths of genocide, tyranny, and impoverishment down which their societies were trending. Before a single socialist regime had established itself, writers including Dostoevsky, W. H. Mallock, and, of course, Kipling glimpsed the horrors that lay concealed within socialism's humanitarian promise. Surely their glimpses into its future in country after country refute the fraying excuse that socialism has never been tried. For if indeed socialism has never been tried, how could they predict its consequences with such eerie accuracy?

# ALL THE BENEFITS YOU'LL NEVER SEE

## French statism has been anything but progressive

**BY PASCAL-EMMANUEL GOBRY**

ONE of Charles de Gaulle's most notorious moments of public wit came when he was asked at a press conference whether "Europe" wasn't the solution to France's problems. After a long defense of his policies, he exclaimed: "Of course, people can jump up and down on their chairs like mountain goats and shout 'Europe! Europe! Europe!' but it means nothing and leads nowhere." It seems that when it comes to health-care reform in the U.S., progressives often think it's enough to jump up and down like mountain goats and shout "France! France! France!" But it's not. I am proudly French, and I have seen the problems of socialism in my nation firsthand.

Let's get the obvious out of the way first: Yes, the French health-care system is, at the moment, almost as amazing as they say. Taking my frighteningly sick daughter to Necker, the main children's hospital in Paris, made me proud to be a French taxpayer. Not only was the building gleaming and everything in it high-tech, but the staff was first-class, efficient, and, above all, kind, a world away from bureaucratic cliché. When, on my way out, after my daughter had recovered, I asked whether I had to pay for anything, the staff looked at me as if I'd just flown in from Mars.

Nonetheless, the French system offers virtually no lessons applicable to the United States.

Progressives either dislike private insurance or want to ban it outright; the French system relies on private insurance. Health-care wonks left and right agree that the biggest problem of the U.S. system is that it is employer-based. French health care? Also employer-based.

Since long-term and so-called lifestyle diseases such as obesity, diabetes, and heart diseases currently pose the biggest threats to public health, progressive health-care wonks are obsessed with preventive care. What's one of the few areas where French health care lags behind the rest of the world? Preventive care.

Another progressive villain is prescription drugs, and France is a notorious over-consumer of them. While progressives are rightly enthralled with the idea of "evidence-based medicine" (while failing to realize that mandating it is sure to bring dysfunction), the French government has found a, let's say, ingenious way to get French people to ingest fewer drugs: It promotes the notorious fraud of homeopathy and, in some cases, even pays for it. The French are also inexplicably obsessed with psychoanalysis, to the point that French mental-health care is essentially stuck in the 1930s. In the name of environmentalism France has long banned genetically modified organisms that science says are harmless for humans and good for the environment, and the government recently bowed to public pressure and passed a partial ban of glyphosate, a herbicide that activists say causes cancer even though scientific studies have found no such link. (Activists say these results are due to a conspiracy; 80 percent of French people support a ban.)

Progressives advocate information technology as a way to make the U.S. health-care system more efficient (again: excellent idea in the abstract, a disaster if you do it via central planning); France is a health-IT laggard.

Progressives routinely point to inequalities in life expectancy between the richest and poorest Americans, often implying that imitating policies such as France's would reduce the difference. The *Washington Post* called the American life-expectancy gap "stunning," and *Vox* blamed it on the Trump tax cuts—really. Such claims imply that America's socioeconomic system is notably bad when it comes to health and death. They don't say it outright, though, because, compared with other OECD countries, the United States is in the middle of the pack for health inequality—right where France is.

So if French health care is so similar to health care in the U.S., how does it manage to have such different outcomes? The answer is that France, with its tradition of state-directed authoritarianism, is able to achieve something that is politically radioactive in the U.S.: severe cost control. France has the lowest doctor pay, relative to average income, in the OECD. A young general practitioner in France made 69,900 euros on average in 2011 (roughly $97,200 at the time), according to the French National Statistics Office. Currently, nurses make 21,840 euros (around $24,300) on average. Despite having to hold the equivalent of a bachelor's degree,

French nurses make 5 percent less than the average income, according to OECD figures.

Which is a natural response to the financial stress on the system. While the French health-care system is presently good, it is also, well, dying. It has its own dedicated tax revenues and spending streams—every year, the French parliament votes on not one budget but two: one for general government and one for health care. The system has been running a deficit every year since 2002. France spends around 11 percent of its GDP on health care every year, which is certainly less than that crazy outlier America but still very high compared with the rest of the OECD. Government spending is already at around 56 percent of GDP, and given EU-imposed budget rules there is not much room to spend more—even as the wave of Baby Boomers is retiring.

Which doesn't leave many options besides squeezing more hours out of already-underpaid workers and cutting benefits. While nurses' salaries stagnate, their working hours keep increasing. According to a survey by the National Order of Nurses, 63 percent of nurses show at least one symptom associated with occupational burnout, and 25 percent have sought psychiatric help as a result of work-related stress. In the health-care utopia of France, 22 percent of nurses polled say they are seriously considering getting into a different line of work.

And there aren't many ways left of decreasing costs. Rural hospitals have been merged, creating so-called medical deserts—large areas with no doctors. In 2017, three years' worth of incident logs from the central teaching hospital in Toulouse, a trove of 26,000 documents, was leaked to the media. Toulouse is a large city known for its picturesque center, nearly year-round Mediterranean sunshine, good universities, a winning rugby team, and being one of the hubs of France's vaunted aerospace industry—all Airbus jets go through final assembly in Toulouse. If you were looking for a place to represent the best of French health care, the teaching hospital in Toulouse would be a top candidate. And yet those incident logs tell a different story.

In a French hospital, each time something unexpected happens, an incident log is filled out. While most of the 26,000 log entries represent the normal imperfections that are found in any organization, "more than a thousand are a sign of poor . . . conditions . . . that can threaten patients' lives," said Sylvain Morvan, editor of the local news site *Mediacités*, which unearthed the documents. Requests to fill holes in the floor received no response for two years. Overweight handicapped patients were left to lie in bed indefinitely for lack of suitable equipment to help them up, leading to further health troubles and depression. In one log, a nurse wrote, "My team is exhausted, physically and psychologically. . . . We feel like we are not doing our jobs well and endangering patients' lives."

There's another way in which the French health-care system stands out: It has the lowest share of out-of-pocket spending in the OECD. There's hardly anyone who doesn't think that has to change; in the immortal words of Barack Obama, "it's arithmetic." Perhaps, say hopeful center-left reformers, more cost-sharing will lead to more competition and innovation, which sounds awfully . . . conservative. The French health-care system has turned out to be a good illustration of Margaret Thatcher's quip that the problem with socialist governments is that sooner or later, "they always run out of other people's money."

With demography putting relentless pressure on costs even as budget constraints mean spending must go down, I always hear the same story from nurses, doctors, and administrators I interview: Yes, right now we are doing okay, but the system will collapse sooner or later.

And that is a story you can tell about the French welfare state in general. As Democratic presidential candidates contemplate proposals such as universal day care and free college tuition, they would again do well to look at France—actual France, not the fantasy of progressive propaganda.

American writers often laud the supposedly wonderful French public day-care centers. In 2013, Pamela Druckerman, the author of *Bringing Up Bébé*, the book that identified a supposedly superior French style of parenting (remember that?), wrote a typical op-ed in the *New York Times* urging America to "catch up with France on day care." As someone who lives in France, has a young child, and has many friends with children, I've certainly heard lots of very nice things about French day-care centers, known as "crèches." But I've yet to meet anyone who has experienced them firsthand. As I wrote back in 2013: "When my wife got pregnant, we duly went to the local crèche office to apply for a spot (well over a year in advance!). When we asked how likely we were to get one, the nice lady simply laughed. She could put us on the waitlist, she said, but that almost certainly wouldn't make a difference."

The French government seems to have given up on trying to make up for the shortfall. Back in 2012, François Hollande was elected president partly on a promise to create tens of thousands of new spots in crèches, but he essentially abandoned that promise on Day One. There are now regular news stories about corruption in the awarding of crèche spots. All of this was predictable: Public provision of important goods leads to rationing and thence corruption.

Pro-family policy has been one of the most ancient and cross-ideological commitments in French politics. France's war defeat by Germany in 1870 was seen as the result of Germany's higher fertility rate, and raising fertility was thereafter considered necessary to win the eventual rematch. Pro-family policy was embraced by the left-wing Popular Front in the 1930s and the Vichy regime in the 1940s, and in the post-war cross-party settlement it was embraced as one of the three "pillars" of France's new welfare state, alongside socialized health-care coverage and redistribution.

This commitment has changed only recently. Obediently following German instructions to reduce the deficit, François Hollande passed unprecedented cuts in family benefits, which now nobody talks about reversing, and the Macron administration occasionally floats proposals for further cuts as a way to balance the budget—to a silence that is striking, given French tradition. Everyone knows why: There's no money anymore.

As for college, far be it from me even to indirectly endorse the insane American higher-education bubble, but every time I cross an American college campus I feel a pang of envy. France does have "free college," of a sort. Its higher-education system is a massively complex tangle of various types of institutions awarding various types of credentials to various types of students. Any high-school graduate (which means, in practice, almost every 18-year-old) is entitled to a spot at a free public university—which makes it odd that private higher education in France is thriving, with close to 20 percent of students going that route. Between 1998 and 2016, private higher-education enrollment grew by 88 percent, as opposed to 14 percent for public higher education.

The explanation cannot be prestige, as might be the case among America's elite universities, since France's most prestigious schools are all public. Nor are private institutions massively subsidized—government funding represents a modest 7 percent of private higher-education institutions' budgets on average.

The answer becomes obvious when you actually set foot in one of those public universities. My top-ranked law school's library, for instance, on top of being crumbling and having Wi-Fi that didn't work most days and only a handful of computer terminals, had a glass wall oriented so that sunlight hit it directly. That wall, combined with a lack of air conditioning and ventilation, turned the library into a locker-room-scented sauna—especially in the spring, which is exam season—with predictable consequences for library attendance.

Then there's the matter of elitism. The world of public universities and professional schools exists apart from the schools that give you a ticket to the French elite. These, the *grandes écoles* (literally, great schools), are where upper-crust parents want to send their children. Unlike public universities, which are open to all high-school graduates, these tiny schools can be entered only via brutal competitive examinations that require two to three years of post-secondary studies. Students who want a shot at the top universities must typically spend 70 to 80 hours a week cramming in an intensely competitive atmosphere, with predictable effects; suicides at the top prep schools are a fact of life, accepted by all.

So it's no wonder that even though there are free public prep schools, students from unprivileged backgrounds cannot compete in them. It's impossible to study 70 hours a week if you also have a long commute, which would be the case for anyone who lives outside the expensive city centers where the best prep schools are. Free universities turn out to be not so much a commitment to social equality as a handout to the plebs so that they don't demand access to the actual paths to elite status.

There is a recurring theme. Somehow, every supposedly progressive French policy turns out to have the same effect: to cement the power of the upper middle class and sap upward mobility. Labor-market regulation is great for *grande école* graduates; it's not so great for the lower-skilled, who must make do with temporary jobs since employers are reluctant to be locked into expensive labor contracts. Housing-market regulations, supposed to protect tenants from abusive landlords, artificially prop up housing prices and subsidize elderly rentiers even as they make it hard for the underprivileged to find housing. And so on down a very long list.

It is difficult to see all this as a coincidence, given that the people who make the rules are those who benefit. Since the election of Emmanuel Macron, more and more observers have become aware that virtually all of France's leadership roles are held by people who went to the same schools and share the same background. Macron describes himself as a progressive, and people like him believe that, owing to their superior education, they have the right to order society for the benefit of everyone. Given the results—low growth, mass unemployment, social strife, and a general mood of pessimism (80 percent of French people believe their children will be worse off than they, the highest rate in Europe)—they might want to rethink their idea of progress.

# BEFORE THERE WAS THATCHER

## Britain's 1970s experiments with statism, and the stagnation they wrought

**BY ANDREW STUTTAFORD**

IF you can remember the 1960s, many are said to have said, you weren't really there. But if Britain fails to remember the 1970s, it may soon find itself in a place where it really should not want to be. Towards the end of the latter, infinitely less entertaining decade, a good number of those at the top of Jeremy Corbyn's opposition Labour party made their political debut as members of a hard Left that was far less of a fringe than it deserved to be. They have come a long way since, but their thinking has not, and with the Conservatives being broken apart by a botched Brexit, Corbyn's own '70s show could be playing in Downing Street soon.

In 1962, former secretary of state Dean Acheson told a West Point audience that Britain had "lost an empire" but "not yet found a role." By the early 1970s it had found one as Europe's latest sick man, made sicker still by new Irish woes. In 1960 the U.K. boasted Europe's most productive economy. Within ten years it had been overtaken by all its major peers. Repeated pressure on its (overvalued) currency signaled that the U.K. was living beyond its means. While Britain's failure to keep up can be partly explained by improving conditions for some of its competitors—a post-war rebound in some cases, long-term laggards pulling themselves together in others—much of the blame was to be found at home. Complacency, systematic underinvestment, mounting trade-union militancy, and (after a Labour government took over in 1964) ever higher levels of taxation and government intervention in an economy already burdened by too much of both, all took their toll. As elsewhere in the West, there was a marked increase in inflation (in Britain's case boosted by a significant devaluation of the pound) in the late 1960s. It handed Ted Heath's Tories a surprise election victory in 1970, but the rising prices were another harbinger that the hitherto chronic British disease was entering an acute phase.

There were early signs here and there, faint foreshadows of what was to come under Margaret Thatcher, that the newly elected Conservatives might be prepared to try something different. Two travel agencies, a brewery, and some pubs were privatized: a start, to be sure, but trivial given that the state-controlled industries still included coal, steel, utilities, and many more besides. There were tax cuts (the top rate of income tax was reduced from 83 to a gentle 75 percent, but—the Tories didn't want to go too far—an additional surcharge on investment income was retained), public spending was trimmed, and the first attempts were made to allow occupants of municipal housing to buy their homes, a policy that the Iron Lady was later to make her own. But despite some free-market talk and legislation to rein in the trade unions, Heath did relatively little to break away from the right-hand lane of the aging statist consensus that was holding the country back.

Even Heath's most notable achievement, Britain's successful application to join the European Communities (the predecessor of the EU), was something that had previously been tried by both Labour and Conservative governments. Heath was a true believer in Europe's "ever closer union," but for the most part, support for British membership (where it existed: the country, then as now, was divided) was essentially transactional. Some were attracted by the thought of new openings for British industry and some by the belief that increased European competition would force the U.K. to raise its game. Others were simply beguiled by visions of joining an "abroad" where life seemed more fun. Deeper concerns about where the European project was going were pushed to one side. They would return.

But Brussels could do nothing to save Heath from the increasingly corrosive effect of Britain's failings on its labor relations. Rising prices, slowing growth, and entrenched class antagonism combined in a way that brought the trade unions new recruits (often, ironically, from across the social divide as white-collar workers looked for shelter from the gathering economic storm) and added a much sharper political edge to their traditional bloody-mindedness (the unions had always enjoyed a powerful position within Labour, a party they helped fund, but this was altogether different). To confront this challenge, the Right needed not only a new approach, but also a substantial constituency to support it. Heath was unwilling to contemplate the first, and the second was several crises away.

With the economy stumbling into stagflation (a new phenomenon by no means confined to Britain), the government turned to an old remedy designed for the stag, but not the flation. It tried to spend Britain's way out of trouble. This led to a brief, unsustainable boom but poured fuel on an inflationary fire that was never likely to be extinguished by the wage and price controls—yet more meddling in the economy—earlier introduced by Heath's intellectually exhausted technocrats. And all the while the strikes, sometimes prolonged, sometimes marked by violence, and occasionally involving massive disruption (the power cuts were not fun, trust me), continued. Britain lost nearly 24 million working days to strikes in 1972 (compared with 300,000 in 2017), owing mainly to the coal miners. When the miners returned to the fray two years later, they brought the Conservatives down. With the country obliged to work a three-day week to conserve power (most of the country's electricity generation was coal-fired), Heath called an election in February 1974 on the issue of "Who Governs Britain."

A weary electorate replied that it didn't know. The Tories won more votes but fewer parliamentary seats than Labour, which formed a minority government. In October, after a few months of comparative calm, Labour gained a higher share of the vote than did the Conservatives and eked out a narrow House of Commons majority. Brits had chosen, they imagined, the option of quietly muddling through, an option that no longer existed.

Radicalism feeds upon itself. The question of who governed Britain was not going away. Emboldened by both a struggling economy (capitalism had failed, you see) and the breaking of the Tories, the hard Left stepped up its campaign to drive Labour in its direction. The trade unions, meanwhile, waited to see how they would be rewarded for their contribution to the Conservative defeat. Neither had too much cause for complaint: The Conservatives' union laws were repealed, taxes on the "rich" reverted to outright looting (a top income-tax rate of 83 percent, rising to 98 percent on investment income), and, at a time when richer, less indebted countries were retrenching in the wake of OPEC's oil shock, public spending soared.

The mid Seventies were hard on most Western economies, but the U.K. appeared to be in a hell of its own. Inflation shot up from over 9 percent in 1973 to more than 24 percent two years later, GDP fell, unemployment rose, the pound crumbled, the stock market crashed, house prices slumped, industry buckled, and some of Britain's best and brightest headed for the exit. In response and with a good degree of union support, Labour's left, including a minister who later would become a mentor of sorts to a young Jeremy Corbyn, agitated for more taxes, more spending, more state control of the economy, and something close to autarchy.

Labour's leadership rejected this path to economic and democratic disaster. Given their political constraints, they did the best they could to connect with economic realism. Spending was cut, a change in direction given wider significance by a speech in which Prime Minister Jim Callaghan appeared to abandon the crude Keynesianism that had characterized so much of British policymaking since the war. Callaghan later claimed that too much had been read into his words, but whatever he meant, spending was slashed still more—this time at the insistence of the International Monetary Fund, the price of a humiliating bailout agreed to in December 1976.

Some have argued that this shift paved the way intellectually and politically for Thatcherism, but it worked so well that for a while it seemed that, despite rising unemployment, the Tories might be held at bay. Inflation fell, tax rates came down (somewhat), public finances improved (low bar), GDP growth picked up (more than a bit). If, as expected, Callaghan had gone to the polls in the autumn of 1978, Labour might even have won. The prime minister balked, but winter—the Winter of Discontent—was coming.

The unions were stirring, pushing back against the government's efforts to hold down pay increases. When these were undermined by the Labour party's left, huge pay demands were followed by a wave of strikes across British industry (from truckers to water workers to the auto sector to the railways to ambulance drivers; take your pick, the list is very long). The chaos was accompanied with images so grotesque—the dead unburied, the sick untreated, the trash piling up in the streets—that they were seared into Britain's political memory for a generation. And so was the government's eventual surrender.

Just a few months later, Margaret Thatcher was in 10 Downing Street, promising change. The Winter of Discontent had sealed the deal for the Conservatives, even if neither the Tories nor their voters had much of a clue what that deal would turn out to mean.

# PRICE NOT, CONSERVE NOT

## Markets are better for the environment

**BY SHAWN REGAN**

As the Soviet Union began to collapse, the socialist economist Robert Heilbroner admitted that central planning had failed economically but said we needed "to rethink the meaning of socialism." Now it was the thing that had to emerge if humanity was to cope with "the one transcendent challenge that faces it within a thinkable timespan." Heilbroner considered this one thing to be "the ecological burden that economic growth is placing on the environment." Markets may be better at allocating resources, Heilbroner thought, but only socialism could avoid ecological disaster.

Not long after, however, it became clear that the socialist economies of Eastern Europe and the former Soviet Union were not just economic failures; they were also environmental catastrophes. Economist Jeffrey Sachs noted at the time that the socialist nations had "some of the worst environmental problems in the entire globe." Air and water pollution abounded. By one estimate, in the late 1980s, particulate air pollution was 13 times higher per unit of GDP in Central and Eastern Europe than in Western Europe. Levels of gaseous air pollution were twice as high as this. Wastewater pollution was three times higher.

And people's health was suffering as a result. Respiratory illnesses from pollution were rampant. In East Germany, 60 percent of the population suffered from respiratory ailments. In Leningrad (now St. Petersburg), nearly half of all children had intestinal disorders caused by contaminated water. Children in Poland were found to have five times more lead in their blood than children in Western Europe. Conditions were so bad that, as Heilbroner acknowledged, the Soviet Union became the first industrialized country in history to experience a prolonged peacetime decline in average life expectancy.

As the Iron Curtain lifted, socialism's dirty environmental secret was exposed: Eastern Europe and the Soviet Union were the most polluted and degraded places on earth. "When historians finally conduct an autopsy of the Soviet Union and Soviet Communism," economist Murray Feshbach and journalist Alfred Friendly Jr. wrote in 1992, "they may reach the verdict of death by ecocide."

Consider the destruction of the Aral Sea between Kazakhstan and Uzbekistan, which has been called "one of the planet's worst environmental disasters." Once the world's fourth-largest inland body of water, it shrank to less than half its original size because of Soviet economic policies. Fixated on making the USSR self-sufficient in cotton production, central planners mandated industrial agriculture throughout the arid region. Massive water diversions for irrigation reduced the sea's inflows to a trickle, causing the biggest manmade loss of water in history. Fishing villages became dry and landlocked. Some, such as the former port city of Muynak, now lie more than 75 miles from the sea.

The desiccation of the Aral Sea also caused severe health problems throughout the region. As the waters receded, the sea's salty floor was exposed, along with pesticides that had accumulated from agricultural operations. All this was then carried by strong winds to nearby communities. Respiratory problems, throat cancer, and other illnesses became more common as the pollutants were deposited in the lungs of millions. The human and environmental consequences are still being felt. Today, infant-mortality rates in the Aral Sea region remain significantly higher than the national average in Uzbekistan, and children there experience similarly high rates of anemia, diarrheal diseases, and other illnesses caused by exposure to toxic contaminants.

How can this be? "Environmental deterioration was not supposed to occur under socialism," Cuban-American researchers Sergio Díaz-Briquets and Jorge Pérez-López wrote in a detailed study of Cuba's environmental legacy. "According to conventional Marxist-Leninist dogma, environmental deterioration was precipitated by the logic of capitalism and its relentless pursuit of profits." Socialism, on the other hand, would avoid capitalism's excesses. "Guided by 'scientific' principles, socialism's goal was a classless and bountiful society," they explained, "populated by men and women living in harmony with each other and the environment."

But this was clearly not the case in the Soviet empire. Nor was it in Cuba, whose environmental record after decades of socialist control was described by Díaz-Briquets and

Pérez-López as "far different from the utopian view." The West, meanwhile, had not only the consumer goods that socialist societies lacked but also a cleaner environment.

One explanation for the disparity is that central planners, unlike markets, grossly misallocate resources, as a matter of routine. Energy prices, for example, were highly subsidized in the socialist economies of Eastern Europe and the Soviet Union. As a result, industrial production was far more energy-intensive throughout the socialist world than in Western European economies—five to ten times higher, according to one estimate—leading to more pollution. A 1992 World Bank study found that more than half of the air pollution in the former Soviet Union and in Eastern Europe could be attributed to subsidized energy pricing during this period.

A related problem was the fixation of socialist planners on heavy industry at the expense of the environment. "The singular dominant fact of the Soviet economic strategy," Jeffrey Sachs has noted, "was the subordination of all human and economic goals to the development of heavy industry." Industrial pollution from factories in Eastern Europe was so bad that *Time* described it as the region "where the sky stays dark." Acid rain in Krakow severely damaged the city's historic structures and buildings, some of which required renovations, and even corroded the faces of many centuries-old statues.

Of course, industry behind the Iron Curtain was anything but efficient, and central planning caused excessive use of natural resources. A 1991 study by Mikhail Bernstam found that market economies used about one-third as much energy and steel per unit of GDP as did socialist countries. Likewise,

Polish economist Tomasz Zylicz found that the non-market economies of Central and Eastern Europe required two to three times more inputs to produce a given output than did Western European economies. (The former Soviet world, as well as China, also emitted several times more carbon per unit of GDP than the United States did—a trend that continues today.) Simply put, market economies make more with less and are therefore better for the environment.

Socialist planners, on the other hand, lack the knowledge necessary to rationally coordinate economic activity. Moreover, bureaucratic constraints make accurate price-setting impossible. In their 1989 book *The Turning Point*, Soviet economists Nikolai Shmelev and Vladimir Popov offered an illustrative example. To bolster the production of gloves, the Soviet government more than doubled the price it paid for moleskin. Warehouses soon filled with mole pelts, but glovemakers were unable to use them all, so many rotted. As the economists explained:

> The Ministry of Light Industry has already requested Goskomtsen [the State Committee on Prices] twice to lower the purchasing prices, but "the question has not been decided" yet. And this is not surprising. Its members are too busy to decide. They have no time: besides setting prices on these pelts, they have to keep track of another 24 *million* prices. And how can they possibly know how much to lower the price today, so they won't have to raise it tomorrow?

Therein lies a crucial flaw in socialist economic logic, and one that has real environmental consequences: Whereas a capitalist firm has ample incentive to act on such information to economize on the use of natural resources, socialist planners have no such motivation—Soviet bureaucracies, Shmelev and Popov noted, were "able only to correct the most obvious price disproportions several years after" they appeared—nor do they have the knowledge needed to accurately set millions of prices at once. And if there are no market prices to convey accurate information about the value of scarce natural resources, there is little chance of conserving them.

Finally, there is the issue of property rights. In a socialist society without them, it is impossible to hold individuals or governments accountable for environmental damages: Planners can increase industrial output without compensating those who bear its costs in the form of pollution. In a capitalist society, property rights offer protection against environmental harms and give resource owners incentives to conserve.

Socialism's environmental record is just as bad elsewhere. As Díaz-Briquets and Pérez-López document, in Cuba, socialists' quest to maximize production at all costs has caused extensive air, soil, and water pollution. And in Venezuela, socialist policies have contaminated the nation's drinking-water supplies, fueled rampant deforestation and unrestrained mining activity, and caused frequent oil spills attributed to neglect and mismanagement by the state-owned energy company.

As socialist ideas capture the American imagination—and are often portrayed, as with the Green New Deal, as necessary to avoid environmental catastrophe—it's important to remember socialism's dismal environmental legacy.

Capitalism may be a dirty word these days, but when it comes to producing the prosperity and creativity necessary to sustain a clean environment, it's still the best system we've got.

# SOCIALIZED MEDICINE IS BAD FOR YOUR HEALTH

## Imagine a shoe store with just one brand of sneakers; now apply that to medical care

BY AVIK ROY

Of all the forms of socialism that persist in the West, socialized medicine may well be the most persistent—and the most consequential.

But first, it's worth defining exactly what "socialized medicine" is, and what it is not. "Universal coverage," a system in which everyone has health insurance, is not necessarily socialized.

Switzerland, for example, has a system of universal coverage in which Swiss residents buy private insurance and receive treatment from private physicians and private hospitals. In contrast to the United States, there are no government-run insurers in Switzerland.

Canada, on the other hand, has socialized, or "single-payer," health insurance, in which the government is the only meaningful health insurer. But Canadian-style socialized health *insurance* is still a minor-league version of socialized health *care*, because single-payer health insurance can—and frequently does—tolerate the existence of privately owned hospitals and physician clinics.

The standard-bearer of truly socialized medicine is the United Kingdom. In Britain, as in Canada, health insurance is the province of the government. But, as it is not in Canada, the *delivery* of health care is also socialized in Britain. That is, a government health-insurance agency pays a government-employed doctor to send Britons to government-owned hospitals.

The British National Health Service was conceived by William Beveridge, a fellow traveler of the Fabian Society, an influential group of British socialists who helped found the Labour party and the London School of Economics. During World War II, the wartime government invited Beveridge to chair a committee that would help plan the post-war British welfare state. His 1942 report to Parliament, *Social Insurance and Allied Services*, argued that "restoration of a sick person to health is a duty of the State . . . prior to any other consideration." He proposed a "compulsory social insurance scheme without income limits" that would establish "a comprehensive national health service [to] ensure that for every citizen there is available whatever medical treatment he requires, in whatever form he requires it, . . . provided where needed without contribution conditions in any individual case."

The British NHS is funded entirely by taxes, and is thereby "free" to patients at the point of care. There are no premiums, no co-pays, no deductibles. In theory, the economic result of such a system should resemble me at an open bar on a *National Review* cruise: excess consumption without respect to need or price. The NHS compensates for this problem in two principal ways: first, by centrally controlling the fees that doctors, hospitals, drug manufacturers, et al. receive for their goods and services; and second, by aggressively restricting the consumption of costly services that would otherwise blow up the British health-care budget.

The aggression and dictation have worked, in a sense. The NHS is kept on a strict budget and has not yet run out of other people's money. In 2013, the United Kingdom subsidized health care to the tune of $3,057 per Briton; by comparison, American-government entities subsidized $4,207 of care per U.S. resident: 38 percent more.

But the NHS is no paradise. Open a random edition of a British daily newspaper and you will likely encounter an article about some egregious problem that the NHS has failed to solve. For example: NHS doctors routinely conceal from patients information about innovative new therapies that the NHS doesn't pay for, so as not to "distress, upset or confuse" them; terminally ill patients are incorrectly classified as "close to death" so as to allow the withdrawal of expensive life support; NHS expert guidelines on the management of high cholesterol were intentionally not revised after becoming out of date, putting patients at serious risk in order to save money; when the government approved an innovative new treatment for blindness in elderly patients, the NHS initially decided to reimburse for the treatment only after patients were already blind in one eye—using the logic that a person blind in one eye can still see, and is therefore not that badly off; while most NHS patients expect to wait five months for a hip operation or knee surgery, leaving them immobile and disabled in the meantime, the actual waiting times are even worse: eleven months for hips and twelve months for knees (compared with a wait of three to four weeks for such procedures in the United States); one in four Britons with cancer is denied treatment with the latest drugs proven to extend life; those who seek to pay for such drugs on their own are expelled from the NHS system for making the government look bad, and are forced to pay for the entirety of their own care for the rest of their lives; and Britons diagnosed with cancer or heart attacks are more likely to die, and more quickly, than citizens of most other developed nations—Britain's survival rates for these diseases are, according to an OECD survey, "little better than [those] of former Communist countries."

One "success" of socialized medicine in Britain is that it has proven impervious to reform. In an attempt to reduce lengthy wait times for emergency-room service, Tony Blair's Labour government introduced a mandate requiring that patients admitted to an NHS emergency room receive treatment within four hours. Some British hospitals responded by instructing their ambulances to drive around town with ailing patients inside, so as to minimize the number of patients technically waiting for care *inside* the emergency room. This year, the NHS announced plans to abandon the four-hour guarantee.

These problems—aggressive limitations on access to care, imperviousness to reform, dishonest statistics—will be familiar to those enrolled in America's homegrown version of socialized medicine: the Veterans Health Administration. As with the NHS, delays and denials of treatment have long been endemic at the VA. In response, the VA installed performance metrics to ensure that veterans were treated without delays; VA hospitals responded by lying on official reports about wait times for treatment.

Understandably, American health-care socialists aren't campaigning on "VA care for all." Instead, their tagline is "Medicare for all," in the hope that Medicare's popularity with seniors can be manipulated to abolish private insurance altogether.

And it is true that the traditional Medicare program is a form of socialized, single-payer health insurance. Indeed, between Medicare, Medicaid, the VA, and other programs, more than 110 million Americans are enrolled in single-payer health insurance today.

It's useful to compare and contrast Medicare with Canada's single-payer system, which by coincidence is also called "Medicare." Canadian Medicare, like the British NHS, makes health care "free" at the point of care, without co-pays or deductibles. Like the NHS, the Canadian system is infamous for its long waiting lists; a 2018 report from the Fraser Institute found that waiting times to see specialists have doubled in the last 25 years; on average, Canadians now wait 20 weeks to see a specialist physician after being referred by their general practitioner. Canadians have long waits not just for treatment but even for basic diagnostic technologies; the average wait time for an MRI scan is 10.6 weeks, and a month for an ultrasound or CT scan. (Wealthy Canadians, of course, have the luxury of being able to hop across the border for needed care, something that nearly all Britons lack.)

American Medicare works in a different way. When Medicare was being designed in 1965, the American Medical Association was concerned that it would lead to federal control over the practice of medicine. Lyndon Johnson, that crafty S.O.B., promised the AMA that if it at least remained neutral about his Medicare bill, he would allow doctors to charge their "usual, customary, and reasonable" rates—that is, whatever they wanted.

Both sides kept their promises, for the most part. American Medicare contains few restrictions on specialist care or expensive technologies. The American Medical Association and other doctors' lobbies, through a secretive group called the "Specialty Society Relative Value Scale Update Committee," effectively determine how taxpayers pay physicians for Medicare services.

These features of Medicare—heavily subsidized premiums and unlimited access—make the program highly popular with seniors. On average, seniors receive more than three dollars in benefits for every dollar they pay into Medicare.

But Medicare's lack of Canadian- or British-style controls has turned the program into an oppressive fiscal burden. Today we spend more on Medicare than we spend on national defense. The program is the biggest driver of our deficits and debt. The Medicare hospital trust fund is already sending out more money than it takes in; according to its trustees, it will run out of other people's money in 2026.

Advocates of so-called Medicare for All are, of course, being dishonest about its unaffordable $30 trillion price tag. But they are also being dishonest about the nature of today's Medicare program. Of the 60 million Americans on Medicare, 22 million are enrolled in a market-based version of Medicare called "Medicare Advantage," in which private insurers compete on price and value to enroll seniors in modernized health coverage, with better health outcomes, lower out-of-pocket costs, and broader benefits than Medicare's single-payer version.

Since 2014, enrollment in traditional, single-payer Medicare has actually declined, from 38.4 million in that year to 38.2 million in 2019. But Medicare Advantage enrollment has soared, from 15.7 million in 2014 to 22.4 million today. "Medicare for All" would abolish these plans, literally ending Medicare as we know it.

Medicare Advantage has rapidly evolved in a way that traditional Medicare cannot, because private insurers tweak their benefits and features in real time, in response to consumer demand. Single-payer Medicare can do that only through acts of Congress and bureaucratic diktats.

Medicare Advantage highlights socialized medicine's biggest lie: that "Medicare for All" expands Americans' health-care "rights." The Anglo-Canadian version of socialized medicine tramples on individuals' rights to seek the care and coverage that they want. The U.S. version tramples on Americans' right to the fruits of their own labor, conscripting them through taxes and debt to fund an unsustainable system.

Health care is indeed a right, in the same way that any use of liberty is a right. And that liberty—to freely seek the care we need, to pay for it in a way that is mutually convenient for us and our doctors, in a system that is sustainable for the generations to come—is one that we must not merely defend, but expand.

# COMMUNITY OF ALL, COMMUNITY OF NONE

## Alienated people are turning to Marx and Ocasio-Cortez

**BY TIMOTHY P. CARNEY**

MODERN conveniences, information technology, and a fairly laissez-faire morality and economy, paired with a decent government safety net, make it pretty easy for Americans to get what they need, in most respects. That makes the rising cry for socialism a bit baffling at first.

But there's a deeper need going unfilled that is driving college students and twentysomethings to their Marx, Engels, Sanders, and Ocasio-Cortez.

And there obviously is something missing in people's lives.

Suicides hit an all-time high in 2017. Opioid deaths are skyrocketing. Even with employers desperate for workers, 7.1 million prime-working-age men remained out of the labor force as of 2016.

Families are forming less often. Americans are increasingly saying they feel like strangers in their own land.

We shouldn't be surprised that people are turning to radical solutions, considering how many are finding modern life in America so wanting. Just because most economic indicators are good doesn't mean this sense of lack is imagined. It turns out there's a lot more to the good life than shows up in the reports of the Bureau of Economic Analysis.

The real reason American socialists are enjoying a moment today is social and cultural poverty. The root cause is something like loneliness. To borrow a term from Marx himself, you could blame alienation.

When I camped out at Occupy Wall Street in 2011, I was most surprised by how little talk there was of bailouts, bank regulations, or really any policy at all. I had come up to New York from Washington, where the nascent Occupy D.C. crowd was complaining about toothless enforcement of the Volcker Rule and the need for a new Authorization for Use of Military Force in our War on Terror.

There were no such hippie wonks in Zuccotti Park. When I asked what their occupation was a protest against, the typical answer was something like "corporate control of government." Then the conversation went like this:

*What do you dislike that corporations are doing with their control of government?*

"Buying politicians!"

*And what are those bought politicians doing that is bad?*

"Silencing the voice of the people."

*Okay, the corporations are in control, the people are silenced, the politicians are bought. They're all in a smoke-filled room. What policies do they pursue or not pursue that you think harm the country?*

"They oppose campaign-finance reform!"

It seemed there was no *there* there. This was a protest about nothing, I thought.

But it was about something. When I counted the signs at Occupy, the most common themes were disenfranchisement and the erosion of democracy.

They were protesting the "hollowing out of democratic institutions," as occupier Rob Eletto put it.

"This is a movement for direct democracy rather than corporatocracy," Sinead Lamel told me during one evening's "General Assembly."

Throughout the day, occupiers took in barn-burning leftist speeches, but the General Assembly was something different. It was all logistics and legislating. It was the formation of a sanitation committee and a library committee. It was debating and passing rules about when the drum circle had to go quiet. It was "direct democracy."

This laborious rule-making was the *point* of Occupy Wall Street, occupier Julia Shindel told me. Having an actual voice in shaping this little society was "extremely intoxicating."

The dream of forming a fledgling civilization in a flagstone-covered park in Lower Manhattan drew many of these left-leaning Millennials to the Occupy encampment in 2011. While the crowds at Zuccotti Park gave up the dream a few weeks later, the same spirit (and many of the same faces) resurfaced in 2015 and 2016 as the Bernie Sanders movement.

At the 2016 Democratic convention in Philadelphia, Berniecrats were as likely to talk about disenfranchisement and democratic revitalization as they were to go on about Medicare for All or "free college." Of course they agreed with Bernie on the policy stuff, but what brought them through the door was the promise that Bernie would give them a voice in politics.

The root cause of both Occupy Wall Street and Bernie 2016 was a prevailing sense of political alienation. Young people felt that they had lost the ability to make a difference in the world, and so they turned to movements that, in addition to peddling a socialist policy agenda, promised political empowerment.

And while both movements placed their hope of reenfranchisement in an impossible dream (believing that, somehow, loud enough protests or restrictive enough campaign-finance regulations would give ordinary people a voice in Washington), the problem they identified was real: Young Americans had lost *agency*, the ability to make a difference, in modern society.

Man is a political animal. We are meant not only to control our own lives but also to shape the world around us. Traditionally, most of us have flexed our political muscle in and through local, mostly voluntary, institutions such as a town government, a parish council, or a PTA chapter. Community institutions have eroded over the decades, though, leaving people without arenas in which to express their political and social nature.

Without a local "political" institution in reach, many young people reached for something that promised enfranchisement and political power. In so doing, they landed in the camps of Occupy and Sanders. Once there, they began singing hymns to Medicare for All, free college, and wealth taxes.

The desperate desire for a political voice in the 2010s has led young people to the far left.

Put another way, modern American society, in which community is weaker and people are more alienated, has proven a fertile ground for socialism.

People need other people. The American Right sometimes neglects this basic fact and ends up deifying the individual or the nuclear family.

When Hillary Clinton wrote, "It takes a village to raise a child," conservatives replied, "It takes a family." Being pro-family is one thing. Denying that child-rearing is in part a community undertaking is another.

Anyone who has raised children knows how that undertaking requires assistance from people outside the nuclear family—in-laws, teachers, coaches, neighbors, religious leaders, and sometimes the neighborhood cops. What connects parents to these figures are institutions. Without these support structures, raising a family is far more difficult.

In wealthy, highly educated neighborhoods, support structures still exist: private schools, strong public schools with involved parents, country clubs, a higher proportion of stay-at-home moms or mothers working part-time, Boy Scout troops, Little Leagues, and so on. In some tight-knit religious communities, such as the Mormons of Utah, or the Dutch Reformed of western Michigan, families can rely on plenty of church-based institutions.

For most of the working class and the poor, though, these institutions are disappearing. People left isolated and alienated find marriage and child-rearing more difficult. The result is more out-of-wedlock births, fewer marriages, fewer children, more divorce.

The political reaction is a demand for a bigger federal safety net.

For instance, the People's Policy Project, a socialist think tank, recently released its "Family Fun Pack," a proposal for a raft of federal programs designed to help poor and working-class people raise families.

The policy paper explains that the capitalist system is not oriented to helping families. "Because income is paid out to the factors of production without any regard for its final family-level distribution," it states, "families with children wind up in dramatically worse financial circumstances than families without children."

The paper then calls for 36 weeks of federally funded paid parental leave, federally funded child care, a federal benefit for stay-at-home mothers, federally funded (and even federally operated) pre-K, and plenty more expansions of the state into the lives of parents and kids.

More and more Democratic politicians will presumably endorse these proposals between now and the 2020 primaries, since many have already proposed socialist policies in other issue areas. And these big-government proposals will have a real constituency.

Two of the ideas undergirding these efforts are correct: The market itself doesn't account for the costs and difficulties of being a parent; and raising a child without help is very difficult, even for married parents with income.

If you read "Family Fun Pack," you come away asking, "How does anyone manage to raise a family without already being rich?" Then you remember: community. Extended family, neighbors, parishes, shuls, civic associations, dinner clubs, swim clubs, and so on. These institutions help families keep their stuff together, help mothers and fathers stay sane, help new parents navigate the daunting path of parenthood.

The erosion of these little platoons has left people seeking a replacement. Socialism is increasingly perceived to be the answer.

Family is just one area where socialism rushes in to fill the void left by the erosion of community. Experience and social science suggest that community erosion increases the demand for regulation.

That is, laissez-faire never worked if it actually meant "anything goes." Instead, strong norms, a sense of duty to one's neighbors, social pressure, and shame have always played a *regulatory* role.

When communities are weaker, these social "regulations" become toothless. That's when government regulations come in.

"In a cross section of countries," four economists wrote in *The Quarterly Journal of Economics* in 2010, "government regulation is strongly negatively correlated with measures of trust."

The causality goes both ways, the study suggests. "Distrust creates public demand for regulation, whereas regulation in turn discourages formation of trust." Put another way, "individuals in low-trust countries want more government intervention even though they know the government is corrupt."

In western Michigan, I saw the flipside of this dynamic firsthand.

When you think of Michigan, you may think of union workers in Detroit and Flint. But western Michigan traditionally has had far lower rates of unionization, while still being dominated by manufacturing and connected to the auto industry. At a McDonald's in Holland, Mich., in April, I asked a couple of retirees why that was.

"A lot of these businesses are started by local people," explained Gary Gunnich over his breakfast, pointing toward the many small manufacturing plants in the small city. Holland is defined by the Dutch ancestry of its residents and the Reformed churches rooted in Dutch Calvinism. The business owners and their workers typically worshiped together on Sundays, Gunnich and his breakfast companion Bill Stehouwer explained. That obviated the need for unionization, he argued.

"A community like this," Gunnich said, "you're not going to screw people over and then survive. It's gonna get out in a hurry."

But fewer and fewer Americans live in a community like that today. More and more live in an alienated landscape where it's more likely that someone will try to "screw people over." When the choice appears to be between getting screwed and getting socialism, it's not a hard call.

The less we're connected to one another via community institutions, and the more isolated we are, the more we grasp for something big to protect us. For young Americans, that's often the state.

# SOCIALISM FOR THE YOUNG AT HEART

## It becomes part of a cherished identity, hopefully not for long

**BY DEIRDRE NANSEN MCCLOSKEY**

THE harsh old joke is that anyone who is not a socialist at age 16 has no heart but that anyone who is still a socialist at 26 has no brain. Myself, I just made it. Tens of thousands of people since the hinge year of 1848 or 1917 or 1968 have loved socialism when adolescents but as grownups have come to detest it, or at best to view it as a puppy love in truth pretty silly.

You can draw for yourself the inference from such biographies. The tens of thousands have all gone the same way, from wanting to "try socialism" to realizing that it has been tried and tried and tried, and failed. The parts of a "mixed" economy that work are the free parts, the Chinese shops and factories as against the state enterprises and the glorious vanity projects of the same state. In the U.S., the private clinics for cosmetic procedures work pretty well. The VA hospitals, one of many socialized parts of U.S. medicine, do not.

Rates of realization vary. Saul Bellow said of his early Trotskyism, "Like everyone else who invests in doctrines at a young age, I couldn't give them up." People come in adolescence to hate the bourgeoisie or to detest free markets or to believe passionately in the welfare and regulatory state. It becomes part of a cherished identity, a faith hard to change.

Yet no one ever starts as a conservative, least of all a classical liberal, by age 16 and becomes a socialist by age 26. Or 36 or 76. Consider what Leszek Kolakowski wrote as a young and disillusioned Pole in 1956, when Communism had shown its hand, in his long list of "what [true, honest] socialism is not." Socialism is not "a state that is convinced that no one could invent anything better" or "a state that always knows better than its citizens where the happiness of every one of its citizens lies." Or consider Robert Nozick, the American philosopher who started as a socialist in his 20s but at age 36, in 1974, penned the libertarian classic *Anarchy, State, and Utopia*. Or consider an earlier crop of converts, such as Arthur Koestler finding darkness at noon, or consider what George Orwell would have concluded had he survived tuberculosis and seen still more of the animal farm of the USSR. Actually existing socialism, as against the actual non-socialism of a place like Sweden, has been of course terrible, right down to Venezuela. It turns out that power tends to corrupt, and absolute power over the economy corrupts absolutely.

And even the romantic ideals of socialism, so appealing to youth, are crazy-inconsistent, as Kolakowski showed in his history of European socialism. They promise a freedom from work that nonetheless makes us rich, a central plan without tyranny, and individual liberties strictly subordinated to a general will. Craaaazy, kids.

Yet, ah, me, how warm the first love for killing people, or at least bossing them around, in aid of Justice and the Revolution. On a British television show in 1994, the brilliant historian Eric Hobsbawm (1917–2012), a lifelong Communist, was asked skeptically by the liberal writer and politician Michael Ignatieff whether "the murder of 15, 20 million people" in the USSR under Lenin and Stalin, a low estimate, "might have been justified" in light of its contribution to founding a Communist society. Hobsbawm *without hesitation* replied, "Yes." Hard-minded. Or party-line-ish. Or thuggish. Oh, Eric.

The saddest people, and the most dangerous if in power, never get over it. Bernie Sanders and Jeremy Corbyn and I are the same age. At 18 we all three had the same idea: "The people's flag is deepest red. / It sheltered oft our martyred dead. / It witnessed many a deed and vow. / We must not change its color now." In 2019, age 77, Bernie and Jeremy retain exactly the same idea they had in 1960. No evidence or inconsistency or unintended consequence matters.

It shows a stubborn pride. "We'll keep the red flag flying here." Hobsbawm describes in his engaging autobiography of 2002 how he wanted to become a Communist at age 14 and became one at 16—though, come to think of it, who would *not* in Germany in 1931, as Eric was, want to become something like a Communist? After all, it looked like liberal innovism was on the rocks. Not anyone with a heart. (By 2002, true, one might inquire about the brain.) Hobsbawm pauses in his book from time to time to explain why, in the face of Stalin's crimes and the suppression of the Hungarian uprising and the rest, he ceased being a dues-paying if unorthodox member of the Communist Party of Great Britain only a few months before it dissolved itself, in 1991. His explanation, a strange one in such an intelligent man, was that he didn't want to give satisfaction to McCarthyites. Faithful to the end, common sense be damned.

It's rather like the atheism at age 16 that bright boys and some bright girls espouse, never to be reconsidered, which then spills out of the mouths of 76-year-olds who have meanwhile not cracked a serious book on theology. Likewise, most of the Marxists and many of the Marxians and Marxoids have not cracked a serious book on economics published after 1867. True, the young "socialists" nowadays have not cracked any books at all, even Marx's. They rely on blog posts by nonreaders.

But why then is socialism so very often that first love, at any rate if you happen to devour in the Carnegie-financed public library of Wakefield, Mass., at age 16, Prince Kropotkin's *Mutual Aid* or John Reed's *Ten Days That Shook the World* instead of *Atlas Shrugged* or *Capitalism and Freedom*?

Two reasons, both testable. For one thing, we all grow up in families, which of course are little socialist communities, from each according to her ability, to each according to his need. Friends are that way, too. Erasmus of Rotterdam started every edition of his compilation of thousands of proverbs with "Among friends, all goods are common." That's right. If you buy a pizza for the party but then declare, "I paid for it, so I get to eat it all," you won't get invited again.

Therefore, when an adolescent in a free society discovers that there are poor people, her generous impulse is to bring everyone into a family of 330 million members. She would not have this impulse if raised in an unfree society, whether aristocratic or totalitarian, in which hierarchy has been naturalized. Aristotle, the tutor of aristocrats, said that some people are slaves by nature. And Napoleon the commissar/pig said, All animals are equal, but some animals are more equal than others. The literary critic Tzvetan Todorov reports that Margarete Buber-Neumann (Martin Buber's daughter-in-law), "a sharp-eyed observer of Soviet realities in the 1930s, was astonished to discover that the holiday resorts for ministry employees were divided into no less than five different levels of 'luxury' for the different ranks of the [Communist] bureaucratic hierarchy. A few years later she found such social stratification reproduced in her prison camp."

For another, as the economist Laurence Iannaccone argues, the more complex an economy becomes, and the further people are, down astonishingly long supply chains, from working with direct fruits, the less obvious are the rewards of their labor. To a person embedded in a large company, and still more to someone in a government office, nothing seems really to matter. Consult the comic strip *Dilbert*. By contrast, a person, even an 18-year-old person, who works on a subsistence farm has no trouble seeing the connection between effort and reward. Saint Paul of Tarsus had no trouble seeing it in the little economy of Thessalonian Christians: "If any would not work, neither should he eat." Such rules are the only way in anything but a highly disciplined or greatly loving small group to get a large pizza made.

Both reasons for youthful socialism seem to have culminated about now in Bernie and Alexandria. We have more and more adolescents without work experience, not living on farms, not living in a slave economy or actually existing socialist economy, and coming still from little societies of family or friends.

The middle-aged socialists, as "The Red Flag" concludes, "keep the red flag flying here." In the U.S., too. Corey Robin, a political scientist at Brooklyn College, wrote recently and warmly about the new socialist fashion among the young: "Under capitalism, we're forced to enter the market just to live. The libertarian sees the market as synonymous with freedom. But socialists hear 'the market' and think of the anxious parent, desperate not to offend the insurance representative on the phone, lest he decree that the policy she paid for doesn't cover her child's appendectomy. . . . Under capitalism, we're forced to submit to the boss."

Uh-huh. And under socialism we're forced to submit to the state and have the identical anxiety, now backed by a gun rather than a checkbook. One is reminded of the other old anti-socialist joke. Under capitalism, man exploits man. Under socialism, it's the other way around.

# PRESERVED IN THEIR POVERTY

## Socialism destroys the human character

### BY THEODORE DALRYMPLE

TRUE socialists do not want a better world, they want a perfect one. That is why they so often view piecemeal amelioration with disdain or even hostility, and why they are willing to sacrifice the happiness of a present generation for the imagined bliss of a generation to come in the distant future. To adapt the Fool's words in *Twelfth Night* very slightly: Present mirth hath no laughter. What's to come is very sure. In delay there lies plenty . . .

If you tell a socialist that hundreds of millions of people have been lifted out of poverty in the last few decades by means the very opposite of those of socialism, he will immediately retort that many millions have also not been lifted out of poverty, as if there had ever been, or could ever be, a time in which all people benefited equally from improving economic conditions, or as if poverty were the phenomenon that needed explanation rather than wealth. Until *everyone* is lifted from poverty, no one should be. Oscar Wilde, in "The Soul of Man under Socialism" (1891), wrote that "it is immoral to use private property in order to alleviate the horrible evils that result from the institution of private property." The only real solution to the problem of poverty, according to him, was the abolition of property itself; and until it was abolished, the person who used his money in this way was the very worst and most dangerous kind of exploiter, for he disguised the fact of exploitation from the exploited by rendering the exploitation bearable.

Wilde's text is in many ways a locus classicus of a certain kind of thought that, though (or perhaps, more accurately, *because*) it is deeply adolescent in nature, retains its appeal in a world that is perennially unsatisfactory to its inhabitants, and not necessarily to the worst-off among them. Wilde—a very clever man, of course—had observed that the character of human beings was not always good but attributed this disappointing fact to the influence of the institution of private property. Abolish private property and "we shall have true, beautiful, healthy Individualism. Nobody will waste his life in accumulating things, and the symbols for things. One will live. To live is the rarest thing in the world. Most people exist, that is all."

This is obviously akin to the Marxist idea that man will become truly himself only after the institution of Communism. What exactly man was until then (which also means what he is now, since Communism has still not been instituted) is not quite clear, but it is nothing very flattering to him, indeed it implies a contempt for the vast mass of humanity past, present, and almost certainly to come. Speaking for myself, I have lived among or ministered to the wretched of the earth for much of my career, but it has never occurred to me for a single instant that they were anything less than fully human, every bit as human and individual as I was myself.

Wilde continues:

> It will be a marvellous thing—the true personality of man—when we see it. It will grow naturally and simply, flowerlike, or as a tree grows. It will not be at discord. It will never argue or dispute. It will not prove things. It will know everything. And yet it will not busy itself about knowledge. It will have wisdom. Its value will not be measured by material things. It will have nothing. And yet it will have everything, and whatever one takes from it, it will still have, so rich will it be.

It seems to me astonishing that anyone could believe such drivel, let alone a man as intellectually gifted as Wilde; but it is far from difficult to find intellectuals who concur, for example Slavoj Zizek, the Slovenian superstar philosopher who is sure to draw crowds of young admirers to his passionate denunciations of the world as it is wherever he goes. It seems that utopian dreamers are like the poor, we have them with us always.

Having denounced the effects of private property on the human personality, Wilde (I take him only as an example) proceeds—in effect like Marx and Engels before him—to imagine the wonderful results that the abolition of private property under socialism will have for personal and intimate relations:

> Socialism annihilates family life, for instance. With the abolition of private property, marriage in its

> present form must disappear. This is part of the programme. Individualism accepts this and makes it fine. It converts the abolition of legal restraint into a form of freedom that will help the full development of personality, and make the love of man and woman more wonderful, more beautiful, and more ennobling.

As it happens, I have closely observed this more wonderful, more beautiful, and more ennobling love of man and woman under conditions, de facto, of socialism, as well as the abolition of legal restraint—that is to say, all legal structure or social obligation in family relations—with its supposedly full development of personality, and it was not quite as lovely as Wilde (or for that matter Marx and Engels) imagined or depicted, to put it mildly. In fact it was appalling, for reasons that surely any moderately sensible person above the age of 20 would have expected and understood. The absence of restraint did not conduce even to liberty, as another Anglo-Irish writer, Edmund Burke, pointed out almost exactly a century before Wilde:

> Men are qualified for civil liberty, in exact proportion to their disposition to put moral chains upon their own appetites; in proportion as their love to justice is above their rapacity; in proportion as their soundness and sobriety of understanding is above their vanity and presumption; in proportion as they are more disposed to listen to the counsels of the wise and good, in preference to the flattery of knaves. Society cannot exist unless a controlling power upon will and appetite be placed somewhere, and the less of it

> there is within, the more there must be without. It is ordained in the eternal constitution of things, that men of intemperate minds cannot be free. Their passions forge their fetters.

Clearly, there is a possibility of intellectual regress as well as progress. The people who lived Wilde's dream whom I saw close up as a doctor working in a poor part of a British city lived under a socialist regime as complete as, though less authoritarian than, that of the erstwhile Soviet Union. Their housing, education, health care, and income derived from the collectivity, not from anything that they did themselves. They lived in the utmost security—the public services would always be there for them—except, perhaps, when they left their homes, when they might be attacked by their peers. It is true that they clung to a certain amount of private property, but it consisted mainly of clothes, a few white goods, the electronic apparatus of mental distraction, and some valueless furniture. Even Wilde could hardly have meant that people should not possess their own clothes; and in fact they lived in an environment that was remarkably equal. Their material standard of living had been successfully dissociated from any effort that they might make.

Their sexual relations were precisely as lacking in legal restraint as Wilde had envisaged. In this respect, he was a prophet; but unfortunately, the rest of his vision was sadly lacking in acuity or verisimilitude. The people being deprived of any economic or contractual reasons for the exercise of self-control and believing they would never be any better- or worse-off if they exerted themselves (except perhaps by crime), relations between the sexes, once subject to restraints of the kind that Wilde wanted removed so that the full beauty of the human personality could emerge, became fluid in the worst possible way. It was unknown for the father to remain present throughout the childhood of his offspring; serial step-fatherhood became a very common pattern. Jealousy, the most powerful instigator of violence between men and women, increased to an astonishing extent. Man was not so much a wolf as a sexual predator to man. Trust disappeared and violence took its place. A social environment was created in which a cycle of relative (if not absolute) poverty, which was a supposed justification for socialism in the first place, now existed as a kind of self-fulfilling prophecy. If socialists so loved the poor that they wanted to preserve them in their poverty, they could hardly have done better.

Socialism is not only, or even principally, an economic doctrine: It is a revolt against human nature. It refuses to believe that man is a fallen creature and seeks to improve him by making all equal one to another. It is not surprising that the development of the New Man was the ultimate goal of Communist tyrannies, the older version of man being so imperfect and even despicable. But such futile and reprehensible dreams, notwithstanding the disastrous results when they were taken seriously by ruthless men in power, are far from alien to current generations of intellectuals. Man, knowing himself to be imperfect, will continue to dream of, and believe in, schemes not merely of improvement here and there but of perfection, of a life so perfectly organized that everyone will be happy, kind, decent, and selfless without any effort at all. Illusion springs eternal, especially among intellectuals.

# FREEDOM IS NOT A TOOL

## Economic liberty is intrinsically good

**BY JONAH GOLDBERG**

*Republican leaders will have to acknowledge that market capitalism is not a religion. Market capitalism is a tool, like a staple gun or a toaster. You'd have to be a fool to worship it. Our system was created by human beings for the benefit of human beings. We do not exist to serve markets. Just the opposite. Any economic system that weakens and destroys families is not worth having. A system like that is the enemy of a healthy society.*

—TUCKER CARLSON, FOX NEWS, JANUARY 2

IN the immortal words of Buffalo Springfield, "There's something happening here, what it is ain't exactly clear."

Carlson is hardly alone. At the precise moment when socialism is mounting something of a new Spring Offensive, many conservatives are abandoning their posts and refusing to defend what was once holy ground. President Trump has helped make protectionism more popular on the right than it has been in generations. Socialized medicine or some near approximation remains unpopular on the right, but it now has advocates of a kind it never had before. At various purportedly conservative publications, the New Deal is back in good odor, as are various notions of "economic nationalism." An editor of *American Affairs* proposes ditching the Left–Right distinction altogether to forge a new "party of the state" that would have conservatives, among other things, embracing the administrative state rather than dismantling it. Both Patrick Deneen's *Why Liberalism Failed* and Yoram Hazony's *The Virtue of Nationalism* (each nominated—along with my book *Suicide of the West*—for Conservative Book of the Year by the Intercollegiate Studies Institute, with Hazony winning) take dead aim at classical liberalism, arguing that the West took a wrong turn when it embraced John Locke.

One is tempted to borrow a line from President Trump and call for a total and complete shutdown of political debates until we can figure out what the hell is going on.

And my friend Tucker is still at it. At the recent National Review Institute Ideas Summit, he again tore into the free market as a "tool" and many of its defenders as tools of a different sort. He conceded that he wasn't necessarily advocating a "different economic system," but he did want more planning. "All I'm arguing for is a clear-sight picture of what the goal is. That's all I'm arguing for. No problem is solved unless you have a very clear image in your mind of what you want the result to be."

Is economic freedom a means or an end? That's the fundamental question here. To put it another way: Is economic liberty simply a form of liberty itself? Is liberty itself a goal, or a tool?

There was a time when the mainstream position on the right was that the goal, at least as it pertains to the role of government, was liberty itself. Not anymore. Many conservatives have grown disenchanted with the arguments for economic liberty, because they see them either as rationalizations for wicked "globalization" or as inimical to various notions of nationalist solidarity.

The answers to these questions (in order: both, yes, both) once united the Right and illuminated the battlespace with the Left. For more than 70 years, the vast majority of conservatives and libertarians have argued that freedom in the economic realm was not just the engine of prosperity (tool) but was also a good in and of itself (freedom!). That is why, until recently, "conservative economist" and "libertarian economist" were largely interchangeable terms. For the Left, tolerance of economic freedom ran along a spectrum—from absolutely none to an at times grudging acceptance or even modest celebration so long as the proceeds from markets funded egalitarian goals.

But this divide goes back farther—even if the labels get murkier. Yuval Levin, in his wonderful book *The Great Debate: Edmund Burke, Thomas Paine, and the Birth of Right and Left*, demonstrates that, in the Anglo-American tradition, one of the defining differences between conservatives and progressives is illuminated by the metaphors they choose. For Edmund Burke and his heirs, the preferred images invoke space. The role of the government is to create a zone of liberty where people may flourish according to their own abilities. The state is like a gardener or a warden who protects his charges but otherwise leaves them alone. For the Burkean, the "statesman's task is therefore not to drive society toward some particular ultimate and just condition," Levin writes, "but to create and constantly sustain a space in which the people may exercise their freedom and enjoy the benefits of life in society." Burke wanted a literal safe space for freedom.

Thomas Paine and his heirs use the language of direction and progress. The government isn't a gardener so much as a shepherd leading his flock to a single destination where all inequities and injustices will be redressed. For Paine this could be achieved only through the blunt application of reason in all things: "It is time that nations should be rational, and not be governed like animals, for the pleasure of their riders." Virtually every progressive or socialist movement shares this worldview to one extent or another. The job for planners is to guide the wheel of history in their preferred direction, toward their preferred destination.

These two orientations, Levin argues, define the progressive version of liberalism and the conservative one: "a politics of vigorous progress toward an ideal goal or a politics of preservation and perfection of a precious inheritance."

First, let me just say, mark me down in the precious-inheritance column.

Second, it is important to concede that the new planners of the Right make some perfectly fine points. No one should worship the market as if it were a religion. Government has a role to play in helping the unfortunate, keeping markets honest, and all that. These are easy concessions to make because they are in fact not concessions but broad statements of common conservative opinion and sentiment.

But at the level of rhetoric, where first principles are formed and clarified, this is all very troubling—and very wrong.

There are two obvious ways to make the case for economic liberty: deductively and inductively. Since we're getting back to basics, let's start with deductive, the way thinkers such as John Locke, Ludwig von Mises, Ayn Rand, Robert Nozick, and, most famously, Milton Friedman did. "Freedom in economic arrangements is itself a component of freedom broadly understood," Friedman wrote, "so economic freedom is an end in itself." The ability to enjoy the fruits of one's own labors is axiomatically a form of liberty. The ability to buy and sell goods within reasonable constraints (variously defined) is obviously a form of freedom. A ban on the sale of firearms may be an infringement of the right to bear arms, but it is first an infringement of the right to spend your own money as you damn well please. As Nozick memorably put it, "the socialist society would have to forbid capitalist acts between consenting adults."

If you take remotely seriously the claim that the pursuit of happiness is an inalienable right, it is almost impossible not to recognize that economic freedom is an irretrievably important component of freedom. To borrow a term beloved by Marxist and libertarian philosophers alike, economic activity is an important point of praxis—where theory is put into real-world action. The careers we choose, the music we play, the cuisines we enjoy, the fashions we embrace, the homes we live in—a linchpin of the "American dream"—all of these things manifest themselves in the economic realm because we so often need to pay for the things we want to do. You can spend your life as a monk, but someone still needs to pay for your books and candles. Many of our other cherished rights are often made possible only via economic liberty. As Friedrich Hayek argued, "there can be no freedom of press if the instruments of printing are under government control, no freedom of assembly if the needed rooms are so controlled, no freedom of movement if the means of transport are a government monopoly." In countries where health care is controlled by the government, the right to life itself is heavily regulated by the state, because it is the state that ultimately decides what treatments and services are rationed.

This idea that the market is just a tool "like a toaster" is profoundly misleading, because it is only a half-truth. Of course the market is a tool. Markets help us make decisions, discover prices, impose efficiencies, drive technological innovation, motivate people to work via the profit motive, and so on. No need to belabor what we can all agree on. But markets are not *just* a tool. Would Carlson wave away the right to bear arms—guns after all are *literally* tools—the way he scoffs at the market? We should not worship guns either, but the right to bear arms, like the right to self-defense, isn't simply a utilitarian concession, it is an inalienable right. Free speech serves as a tool every bit as much as markets do. The dissemination of knowledge, holding government accountable, taking in ad dollars for prime-time cable shows: The right to free speech makes all of these things possible. But is it just a tool?

Then there's the inductive case. Carlson says that "no problem is solved unless you have a very clear image in your mind for what the result should be." In ways large and small this is untrue. In our personal lives, many of the greatest things—the best solutions, often to problems we could articulate only in hindsight—were found through a process of discovery. From whom we love and marry to our favorite books, music, food, and friends to the vocations we dedicate our lives to—these are not the culmination of some plan. Science is many things, but without the benefits of accidental discovery, of pursuing blind curiosity, the volume of its accomplishments would be dismayingly slimmer. Parenthood is often a source of great joy; those joys are only rarely and intermittently the product of grand plans coming together.

Likewise, no one planned capitalism. It was in a very significant sense an accidental by-product of the quest for liberty, knowledge, and peace. The Calvinists described by Max Weber in *The Protestant Ethic and the Spirit of Capitalism* did not develop their theology to get rich, they got rich because of the changes of habit and custom their theology required of them. Religious pluralism itself wasn't the plan, it was a compromise after a century of war. As the historian C. V. Wedgwood put it, the West came to understand "the essential futility of putting the beliefs of the mind to the judgment of the sword." Religious freedom yielded new freedoms—to innovate not just theologically but economically. Trade itself is an innovative compromise that allowed us to get past zero-sum acquisition by force in favor of mutually beneficial exchange. The market creates peace and freedom by allowing strangers to interact without resort to violence.

Tilt your head just slightly and the historical record shows the causal arrows pointing in a different direction. Economic liberty created a demand for political liberty. Locke, both hailed by many and now vilified as the father of liberalism, was a devout, if idiosyncratic, Christian of Calvinist roots who believed economic liberty to be the keystone of liberty itself. The right to private property, including the ownership of one's own life and body, and the right to own the fruits of one's own labors, is what made freedom not simply possible but morally necessary and even divinely mandated. "The state of nature has a law of nature to govern it," he wrote, "which obliges every one: and reason, which is that law, teaches all mankind, who will but consult it, that being all equal and independent, no one ought to harm another in his life, health, liberty, or possessions." There are sound conservative objections to Locke, originally formulated by Willmoore Kendall in 1941. Locke was a passionate individualist but also a believer in unfettered majority rule. Kendall identified the explanation for this seeming inconsistency: He believed that humans by nature were moral and rational. Locke's anthropological assumption is certainly worthy of debate.

But whichever way you come down on the integrity of Locke's philosophy, the historical fact is that it served as a powerful weapon against notions of aristocracy and the divine right of kings. And the rising middle class—the bourgeois burghers and businessmen—of Western Europe used these ideas, as well as those of the liberal French philosophes, to press for greater and greater political liberty as a means to secure their economic freedom. As their ranks swelled, so did the coffers of the tax collectors, which led to even more demands not just for greater representation but for neutral rules set apart from the whims of rulers and from the hereditary prerogatives of aristocrats. "Historical evidence," Friedman observed, "speaks with a single voice on the relation between political freedom and a free market."

This points to the importance of rhetoric, which Wayne Booth defined as "the art of probing what men believe they ought to believe." Locke's analysis may leave room for serious correction, but the ideas he represented put the West and the world on a path toward freedom and prosperity. Changing what men ought to believe, as history has shown countless times, can take them off the path.

Consider the rule of law. As a component of liberalism, the "rule of law" is often listed as separate from "limited government," and in some cases rightly so. But the rule of law is synonymous with limited government in another sense. When the rules apply the same to rulers and ruled, the arbitrary power of the state is curtailed. Defending free markets, often over the objections of monied interests seeking to rig the system in their favor, is indispensable to protecting freedom in general. For when the state is captured by factions, they will not stop at regulating economic arrangements alone.

This points to the real problem with the new crisis in confidence in the free market. It's an attack on the wrong problem. Many a new fan of statism on the right has convinced himself that "globalists," "elites," "cultural Marxists," or some other "neoliberal" cabal has rigged the system in its favor. In some specific cases, it is an understandable and defensible proposition. The problem arises when the inference is turned into a systemic indictment and the system in the dock is the market. The villain is not the market but the state. More specifically, the interests that capture the state, or mechanisms of it, are to blame. That isn't the free market.

In *The Wealth of Nations*, Adam Smith wrote that "people of the same trade seldom meet together, even for merriment and diversion, but the conversation ends in a conspiracy against the public, or in some contrivance to raise prices." This line has been quoted by critics of capitalism in all parties since 1776. They ignore what Smith went on to say. "It is impossible indeed to prevent such meetings, by any law which either could be executed, or would be consistent with liberty and justice. But though the law cannot hinder people of the same trade from sometimes assembling together, it ought to do nothing to facilitate such assemblies; much less to render them necessary."

Smith's point was the same one addressed exhaustively in *The Federalist Papers*: faction. Whether it's banks or government unions, sugar farmers or the higher-education lobby, the most enduring threat to freedom, economic or otherwise, comes from factions' seeking to marry the state to their narrow interests or agendas. Capitalism emerged in England in part because the king was weak and competing sources of power had to be accommodated. That's how the Magna Carta was born. Nobel-prize-winning economist Douglass North demonstrated that the more diversely power is distributed in a society, the more the different institutions holding power are incentivized to agree to neutral rules that are fairly enforced for everyone. The more healthy institutions you have, the more room there is for other institutions to rise up, and the greater the number of opportunities that emerge for individuals to discover new sources of meaning and avenues to pursue happiness. Joseph Schumpeter demonstrated that monopolies can't endure in a free market—if they do not have the protection of the state. Monopolies are the goal not simply of trusts and combines but of every faction convinced that its interests deserve special dispensation from the state or devoted to the idea that its vision of society should be binding on everyone.

For millennia the vast majority of human beings were poor and unfree because a handful of interests symbolized by the throne, the altar, the guild, or the sword used its power to stifle innovation in any form, because innovation is always a threat to the established order. Order is both good and valuable, when it is just. But too much order stifles innovation, and innovation—which is possible only where there is the freedom to innovate—is the indispensable wellspring of economic growth, material prosperity, and the pursuit of happiness. The Founders understood this, which is why, prior to the ratification of the Bill of Rights, the word "right" appeared in the Constitution only to protect intellectual property: "to promote the Progress of Science and useful Arts, by securing for limited Times to Authors and Inventors the exclusive Right to their respective Writings and Discoveries."

Those who think that the solution to our problems lies in granting the government even greater power to "plan" how people should live are not merely making Friedrich Hayek cry, they are no doubt unwittingly following the path of every enemy of freedom since freedom was conceived as right for all, not just those at the helm. They may couch their appeals in the language of populism, socialism, or nationalism and defense of the common folk. But they invariably have in mind only one slice—their slice, their faction—of the public as truly deserving. "Believe me, sir," Burke writes, "those who attempt to level never equalize. In all societies, consisting of various descriptions of citizens, some description must be uppermost."

# THE INDUSTRIAL MIRACLE

## When the world stopped having to be poor

BY MARIAN L. TUPY

OUR species is 300,000 years old. For the first 290,000 years, we were foragers, subsisting in a way that's still observable among the bushmen of the Kalahari and the Sentinelese of the Andaman Islands. Even after *Homo sapiens* embraced agriculture, progress was painfully slow. A person born in Sumer in 4,000 b.c.e. would find the resources, work, and technology available in England at the time of the Norman Conquest or in the Aztec Empire at the time of Columbus quite familiar. Then, beginning in the mid 18th century, many people's standard of living skyrocketed. What brought about this dramatic improvement, and why?

Our story has to begin with income, for, as Oxford economist Paul Collier has noted, economic "growth is not a cure-all, but lack of growth is a kill-all." The history of economic growth, as Angus Maddison and his team at the University of Groningen found, resembles a hockey stick. For thousands of years, growth was negligible. This period is represented by the shaft of the stick. Toward the end of the 18th century, however, economic growth started to accelerate, first in Great Britain and then in the rest of the world. The blade represents this sharp upward turn.

As measured in 2011 U.S. dollars, the global income per person per day in the first year of the Common Era stood at $2. That's also where it stood when William the Conqueror set sail in 1066 to claim the crown of England. This income stagnation does not imply that no economic growth happened over that approximate millennium. Growth did occur, but it was low, localized, and episodic. In the end, the gains always petered out.

In 1800, the average income was $2.80. In the 18 centuries that separated the emperorship of Caesar Augustus and the presidency of Thomas Jefferson, per capita income rose by less than 40 percent. Again there were regional differences, but they were not great. At the start of the 19th century, average Americans and Britons were twice as prosperous as the global average, roughly speaking

Then industrialization changed everything. Between 1800 and 1900, GDP per person per day doubled. In other words, income grew over twice as much in one century as it had over the preceding 18 combined. By 2016, the number had risen to $40. In the United States, it stood at $145, and in Africa, the world's poorest continent, at $13. In other words, global and American standards of living rose twelvefold and 24-fold respectively over the course of the last two centuries.

Global income per person per day rose at a compounded rate of about 1.8 percent per year over the last hundred years. It will reach $166 per person per day in 2100—if the trend continues. In the United States, it will reach $605 per person per day.

One might object that GDP figures are not the same as take-home pay. Unfortunately, a global hourly wage is tough to calculate—people work different numbers of hours, economies are composed of different kinds of workers, the proportion of non-wage compensations differs, etc. But we do know how American workers fared over the course of the last 200 years.

According to Lawrence H. Officer of the University of Illinois at Chicago and Samuel H. Williamson of Miami University, nominal hourly wages of unskilled U.S. laborers increased 31,627 percent between 1800 and 2016. The nominal hourly compensation of production workers rose 79,775 percent over the same time period. Adjusting for inflation, Gale Pooley, an economist at Brigham Young University, Hawaii, estimates that production-worker compensation rose by a factor of 40.2, and unskilled wages by a factor of 16.3, between 1800 and 2017.

What was responsible for these unprecedented improvements? Scholars offer different, though related, explanations. The Nobel-prize-winning economist Douglass North argues that the evolution of institutions including constitutions, laws, and property rights was instrumental to economic development. Deirdre Nansen McCloskey, an economist at the University of Illinois at Chicago, attributes the origins of the "great enrichment" to changing attitudes about markets and innovation. Harvard University psychologist Steven Pinker contends that material and spiritual progress are rooted in the Enlightenment and the concomitant rise of reason, science, and humanism.

Whatever its exact causes, the Industrial Revolution, which started in the mid 18th century, brought widespread changes, including new fuels, such as coal and petroleum; new motive power, such as the steam engine and the internal-combustion engine; new machines, such as the spinning jenny and the power loom; and the factory system, which reorganized work and required much greater division of labor and specialization of function. These changes increased the use of natural resources and enabled the mass production of manufactured goods.

The Industrial Revolution also led to fundamental non-economic changes. Improvements in agricultural productivity allowed a larger population to eat. That, along with new opportunities for factory work, increased urbanization and contributed to the development of political awareness among the "lower orders." At the same time, wealth became more widely distributed, as landed interests gave way to the interests of the nouveau-riche bourgeoisie. All in all, old patterns of authority were eroded and society became more democratic.

Important political developments, such as the liberalization of trade, allowed the benefits of industrialization to spread globally. Trade volumes rose and, through the process of price convergence, costs fell. The gold standard and the invention of the telegraph made capital transfers easier. Attracted by higher profits, investment flowed from more developed to less developed countries.

Income growth, it is true, is only one of many indicators of human well-being. After all, Alexander the Great, who was the richest and most powerful man in the world, died at the age of 32 from typhoid fever—a disease that is easily curable today. But a wealthy society can support more scientists, pay for advanced medicine, and build better sanitation infrastructure. Wealth makes (almost) everything easier.

It is noteworthy that income growth over the last two centuries went hand in hand with other salutary developments.

As late as 1870, life expectancy in Europe, the Americas, and the world was 36, 35, and 30 years. Today, it is 81, 79, and 72 years.

In 1820, 90 percent of humanity lived in extreme poverty. Today, less than 10 percent does.

In 1800, 88 percent of the world's population was illiterate. Today, 13 percent of the world's population is illiterate.

In 1800, 43 percent of children died before their fifth birthday. Today, less than 4 percent does.

In 1816, 0.87 percent of the world's population lived in a democracy. In 2015, 56 percent did.

In 1800, food supply per person per day in France, which was one of the most advanced countries in the world, was a mere 1,846 calories. In 2013, food supply per person per day in Africa, the world's poorest continent, amounted to 2,624 calories.

Conflict, which was the default state of humanity for millennia, has declined. In the early 1800s, the combined military and civilian death rate from conflicts was about 65 per 100,000 people. By 2000 that rate had fallen to about two per 100,000. The last great-power conflict, which pitted

China against the United States over the future of the Korean Peninsula, ended in 1953.

Slavery, which was rampant in most parts of the world in 1800, is now illegal in every country.

Finally, for the first time since the start of industrialization, global inequality is declining as developing countries catch up with the developed world. Between 1990 and 2017, argues Branko Milanovic from City University of New York, the global Gini coefficient, which measures income inequality among all of the world's inhabitants, decreased from 0.7 to 0.63.

Today, it is de rigueur to focus on the negative aspects of industrialization, but contemporary observers understood that they were living at a time of unprecedented improvement in the human condition. Karl Marx and Friedrich Engels observed in *The Communist Manifesto* (1848):

> The bourgeoisie, during its rule of scarce one hundred years, has created more massive and more colossal productive forces than have all preceding generations together. Subjection of Nature's forces to man, machinery, application of chemistry to industry and agriculture, steam-navigation, railways, electric telegraphs, clearing of whole continents for cultivation, canalization of rivers, whole populations conjured out of the ground—what earlier century had even a presentiment that such productive forces slumbered in the lap of social labor?

If progress is to continue, it is vital that people throughout the world, including socialists in America, better understand the vast extent of the improvements in human well-being over the last two centuries and the reasons for those improvements.

# FREE THE MARKET, FREE YOUR MIND

## Or, Stalin was a bureaucrat

BY KEVIN D. WILLIAMSON

THE main question of capitalism-vs.-socialism isn't efficiency, market incentives, or competition—it is: Who has the power?

Workers in the capitalist world sometimes feel powerless in comparison with their employers, but they have the power to exit that relationship and take a different job, as millions of workers do every year. But imagine if there were only one employer.

Leon Trotsky was in many ways a critic of the Soviet police state—whose leaders eventually had him murdered for that criticism—and one of his observations is of enduring interest at this moment in history: Under socialism, an energetically active police state is, eventually, superfluous.

> During the "purgations" in the last month of 1935 and the first half of 1936, hundreds of thousands of members of the party were again expelled, among them several tens of thousands of "Trotskyists." The most active were immediately arrested and thrown into prisons and concentration camps. As to the

> rest, Stalin, through *Pravda*, openly advised the local organs not to give them work. In a country where the sole employer is the state, this means death by slow starvation. The old principle: who does not work shall not eat, has been replaced with a new one: who does not obey shall not eat.

And here is a sentence that you don't read very often: Leon Trotsky and F. A. Hayek saw this issue much the same way. Hayek wrote:

> That the freedom of the employed depends upon the existence of a great number and variety of employers is clear when we consider the situation that would exist if there were only one employer—namely, the state—and if taking employment were the only permitted means of livelihood. . . . A consistent application of socialist principles, however much it might be disguised by the delegation of the power of employment to nominally independent public corporations and the like, would necessarily lead to the presence of a single employer. Whether this employer acted directly or indirectly, he would clearly possess unlimited power to coerce the individual.

But socialism as such was, in Hayek's mind, not the only threat taking this form. As I explore at some length in my forthcoming book, *The Smallest Minority*, Hayek worried that the emergence of salaried corporate employment as a nearly universal household norm would diminish the liberty previously enjoyed by the class of affluent sole proprietors and those we used to describe as "independently wealthy."

The habits of corporation life—bureaucracy, conformity, the managerial mindset—were, he feared, likely to become dominant cultural trends, a consideration touched on by other roughly contemporary authors ranging from William Whyte in *The Organization Man* to Erich Fromm in *Escape from Freedom*. Hayek's rather forthright elitism distinguishes his approach from that of the Marxist-Freudian critic Fromm, but the clear-eyed journalist Whyte came to similar conclusions in his work on corporate research-and-development programs: Society needs a relatively independent class of free thinkers who are not immediately answerable to a committee of managers and the tut-tutting minions of "human resources," an appellation that to me has always sounded entirely dystopian.

At our particular moment in history, those who describe themselves (risibly and inaccurately) as the partisans of "social justice" have taken up Stalin's task, empowered partly by new technologies such as social media (particularly Twitter) and by old-fashioned partisan-hack activist organizations such as Media Matters, with the goal of cultivating a kind of moral hysteria that can be used to bully the ever-sensitive managers of corporate America into acting as a single employer for political purposes, achieving in the capitalist form the socialist goal of using employment as an instrument of political discipline. The university has been similarly hijacked—College Man is only Corporation Man in larval form—in order to exclude those with nonconforming political tendencies from the mainstream of elite economic and social life.

At the moment, the grim prospect that this campaign will prove broadly successful appears likely. Part of the reason for that is that the independently wealthy elites of our time are less interested in Hayekian intellectual independence and more inclined to seek Fromm's "escape from freedom." The corporate leaders at firms such as Facebook, Google, and Apple are, in spite of their vast wealth, in practice easier to bully than is the average midwestern car dealer or bank president with relatively little professional interest in or exposure to politics. Mark Zuckerberg is so beaten down by the fact that his monolithically progressive peers in California blame him—not just his platform, *him*—for Donald Trump's election as president in 2016 that he has found the emotional and moral energy for a comprehensive reorganization of Facebook's business model and practices. Facebook in particular seems vulnerable to bullying of this kind, which is one of the reasons why the company takes relatively little interest in the propaganda of politically acceptable anti-Semites such as Louis Farrakhan but recently announced a crackdown on anti-vaccine activists and their speech. It's not the kookery but how the kookery makes progressives feel that really matters.

But there are reasons to be hopeful, too. Instruments such as Facebook and Twitter have empowered partisan hate-mobs and taken a few scalps in the process. That kind of thing is a regular occupational hazard for professional controversialists such as Tucker Carlson or Bret Stephens (or me), a cost of doing business, more or less. It is much more significant for previously obscure fast-food workers and Starbucks managers who lose their jobs in impromptu social-media crucifixions. But at the same time, Internet-based forms of communication have provided important, irreplaceable outlets in places where liberal free-speech and free-press regimes are not the norm, including places such as the Middle East and China where the tech giants have, to their shame, subordinated themselves to various despots.

And there are signs of life in the economically liberated class of Hayekian independents. It has proved relatively difficult for the social-justice Left to bring to heel such non-conformists as Whole Foods founder John Mackey, who was targeted for his criticism of the Affordable Care Act, or billionaire venture capitalist Peter Thiel, whose embrace of the Trump administration infuriated many of his peers. Amazon's Jeff Bezos is at war on three fronts: The Left resents the fact that his *Washington Post* has opened up a little bit more to conservative and libertarian voices and blames him for it; the Trump administration hates him like poison, and the president himself has suggested using tax law as a political weapon against Amazon in retaliation for the *Post*'s bitterly critical coverage of his larks and shenanigans; and Bezos has created unnecessary trouble for himself with the irregularity of his personal life, which has attracted the interests of the *National Enquirer*, whose current owners (it is up for sale as of this writing) are closely allied with the Trump administration.

Bezos has proved a particularly difficult man to lean on. When the *Enquirer* threatened to publish embarrassing photographs of a personal nature, Bezos responded not with litigation but with an open letter denouncing what he described as obvious blackmail. Bezos, who is the world's wealthiest man on any given day depending on the volatility of Amazon shares, is the very model of a Hayekian independent: "If in my position I can't stand up to this kind of extortion, how many people can?" he wrote. "On that point, numerous people have contacted our investigation team about their similar experiences with AMI, and how they needed to capitulate because, for example, their livelihoods were at stake."

Sales in Amazon's North American division rose 33 percent in 2018, to $141 billion, and the company realized more than $10 billion in profit—a chief executive delivering that kind of performance can endure the disclosure of a few cringe-inducing, lovelorn texts to his mistress. Even with his net worth getting dinged a little in the divorce, he is effectively untouchable.

The Mark Zuckerbergs and Tim Cooks of the world could be liberated, too, if they chose to be. The purportedly "failing" *New York Times*, which made a respectable profit in 2018 and added more than 100,000 paid digital subscribers, has proved remarkably resistant to hate-mob efforts from the left and from the right targeting hires such as Bret Stephens and Sarah Jeong. Institutional character matters: Yale folded in the face of a hate-mob attack on Erika and Nicholas Christakis, but little ol' University of the Arts in Philadelphia stood tall when students demanded the firing of Camille Paglia for her nonconforming views on transgender issues, dismissing viewpoint retaliation out of hand. As Facebook takes on more and more of an editorial role—its claims of being a mostly neutral "platform" whose managers intervene only in the interests of community standards and "safety" are very difficult to take seriously—Zuckerberg et al. will face much the same test.

If they fail that test, which seems likely, then there are others who will step in and get into the Internet-based/social-media publishing game, which has relatively low barriers to entry (Facebook and Twitter's main advantage in the marketplace is not technology, capital, or—least of all—managerial excellence, but simple *path dependency*, which can be overcome, as Facebook itself once demonstrated against MySpace), and find profits in what we might as well call *samizdata*, given the resurgence of socialism in U.S. political discourse. In much the same way that Elon Musk managed to exnihilate a fantastic automobile company that most critics believed had no organic reason to exist (Tesla faces its challenges, to be sure, but what it already has achieved is remarkable, and Musk can already claim a place next to Henry Ford's in automotive history), media entrepreneurs such as Joe Rogan have brought into being enormously popular and influential models of communication even in the face of corporate competitors and political enemies who would, if they had the power, exclude them from the public square and the marketplace.

The fact is, we love our high-achieving scoundrels, our dissidents, and our nonconforming geniuses. People may respect Bill Gates, but they loved Steve Jobs. You'd let Lee Iacocca babysit your kids, but you'd rather go out and have a drink with Elon Musk. The better sort of person enjoys (and maybe even admires) Musk's SEC-baiting and dramatics more than he resents them. We can look past Henry Ford's horrifying bigotry to see what was best about the man, even as we understand that the madness of Howard Hughes and his genius were a package deal. And therein lies a truth that is too seldom genuinely understood or appreciated: What we call "capitalism" is not, and never has been, primarily about the bloodless pursuit of a slightly better profit margin. The business of business is important—it is necessary—but the best part of capitalism is, and always has been: *joy*.

Do you know what Steve Jobs did not need before returning to Apple and what Elon Musk did not need before starting Tesla? A paycheck. They wanted to do something cool, to create something new and delightful and previously unknown. All of the apparatus of American capitalism—our superlative institutions of higher education and the annual crops of engineers and scientists they produce, the financial operators and venture capitalists, the mind-bendingly complex infrastructure and logistical expertise behind the integration of global supply chains—finds its highest expression in serving those ends. It is almost impossible to imagine that what gets Jeff Bezos out of bed in the morning is the desire for an extra billion dollars or two. The genius of American capitalism in particular is that American capitalism is cool. The Germans build fine stuff, and the Chinese build pretty good stuff pretty inexpensively, but what's the *coolest* German company? BMW? Leica? With the exception of a few high-design/high-tech firms such as Japan's Sony, along with Europe's enduring fashion powerhouses, the cool stuff comes from California garages, Boston laboratories, Austin dorm rooms, Brooklyn home offices . . .

Which is to say: It is the intersection of big ideas, big innovation, and (very often) big personalities with all that ordinary stuff we call "capital" that makes the magic happen. Among other reasons, that is why the urban centers where big ideas meet big money produce so much world-changing innovation relative to the less densely populated rural areas, even though the *politics* of the big cities are, in theory, less enthusiastic about capitalism per se. New York City and the Bay Area are not the best-governed places in the United States, but the success of the enterprises that call these places home is proof of what really makes capitalism work: You can't keep a good idea down. Not forever.

That redounds to the benefit of profit-seeking enterprises and crusading entrepreneurs, but also to the benefit of patronage-dependent artists and intellectuals, nonprofit cultural and artistic institutions, public-policy and activism groups, and enterprises, including political magazines (such as this one), that are not oriented toward fattening up the margins. Companies such as Google spend tremendous amounts of money on projects that have little or no prospect of near-term profitability. Part of that is the "portfolio" model of innovation: Because you cannot pick out the blockbusters in advance, you have to invest in a lot of different areas, catching a lot of little fish as you fish for the big ones. But much of this is sustained simply by the desire to put all of that capital and innovation to work doing something cool. It is precisely the largeness of spirit of American capitalism—which is not defined by the nickel-and-dime mentality regnant down there in accounting—that makes possible this joyful pursuit of the new, the cool, the excellent, the innovative, the delightful.

Adlai Stevenson famously put it this way: "My definition of a free society is a society where it is safe to be unpopular. Where it's safe to say what's on your mind, especially when everyone disagrees. Where it's safe to believe what you believe, especially when everyone else's beliefs stand elsewhere." The Left has for the past decade or so been on a jihad to abolish Adlai Stevenson's free society, to ensure that it is unsafe—often literally, physically unsafe—to hold unapproved political ideas. The fact that the Left has had some success in this endeavor is dispiriting, and it speaks ill of certain institutions—the universities, some of the New York City book publishers, and the Silicon Valley technology firms being tragically prominent among them. But we also have seen limits on the ability of the Twitter mobs—and the president of the United States of America—to silence critics or exclude certain voices from the public discourse. Inevitably, that includes some terrible voices: Islamic extremists, white nationalists, Communists, fashionable anti-Semites, etc. Not long ago, that was understood as both the price and the purpose of a tolerant culture: Rights such as those acknowledged in the First Amendment serve not to protect the speech we find acceptable but precisely the speech we find most objectionable, offensive, or even immoral. Our political culture has, partly and one hopes temporarily, lost touch with that.

But capitalism has provided the tools to subvert much of that forcible conformism while maintaining a culture that still rewards innovation and excellence over bureaucracy and obedience. Though the advice would not have served recent Apple investors very well, there is some truth to the Wall Street proverb about shorting a company's stock when it decides to build a new headquarters building: Once a business ceases to be a campaign and ossifies into a committee, it is dead, even if it continues to throw off some profits for a long time after.

# TIMING IS EVERYTHING

## The economy over the decades

**BY RAMESH PONNURU**

SOMETHING feels off in the timing of our debate over the economy. A loss of faith in free markets, among intellectuals and the public alike, was only natural in the 1930s. But today? Intellectuals on the left and the right are more convinced than ever that our economic policies are deeply misguided, at the same moment that unemployment rates and wage growth are the best they have been in decades. When Americans answer polls, they express less and less confidence in free-market capitalism—even as they express more and more satisfaction about economic conditions.

Perhaps people are evaluating these questions against different time horizons. They may, that is, think that the economy is performing well at the moment but has become less capable of delivering broad-based prosperity over the course of a generation. If today's conditions persist long enough, then, the reputation of capitalism may recover.

Timing is relevant to our evaluation in another way. If our economy has gotten worse at generating sustained prosperity, worse enough to make a loss of faith in capitalism understandable if not justified, then it matters when this decline began.

In 2015, during the last presidential campaign, Hillary Clinton suggested that "for decades" the economy had been offering a worse deal for most people. Her explanation: "For 35 years, Republicans have argued that if we give more wealth to those at the top—by cutting their taxes and letting big corporations write their own rules—it will trickle down. It will trickle down to everyone else." The election of Ronald Reagan, in other words, was the turning point. It followed that many of his policies should be reversed: The top tax rates should go back up and unions should be strengthened.

If economic conditions have been deteriorating for an even longer period, however, then merely reversing Reaganomics might not be enough. And it is common to run into claims, apparently backed by data, that suggest as much. The Pew Research Center notes that the average wage, adjusted for inflation, fell between 1973 and 2018. It had risen steeply from 1964 (when the data series began) through 1973. Then it dropped for roughly two decades, and over the next two recovered but did not get back to its peak.

If real wages have truly been stagnant for longer than most Americans have been alive, then the economy has not worked in anything resembling the fashion we expect. Economic growth has been mostly an illusion: We have more stuff only because more of us work, large numbers of women having joined the paid labor force. If this picture is accurate, we need to make radical changes either to the economy or to our expectations of ever-rising prosperity.

There are, however, two big reasons to doubt the stagnation thesis. The first is that non-wage benefits have become a larger and larger element of compensation. Perhaps they have become too large an element: The tax code encourages employees to get health insurance through their companies rather than take higher wages and buy coverage themselves, and there are reasons to think we would be better-off if the tax code did not do that. But non-wage benefits have economic value to employees, and so looking at wages alone will cause us to underestimate employees' material welfare.

The second reason for doubt is that a common method of adjusting for inflation—the one used in the Pew numbers cited above—overdoes it. The center-right social scientist Scott Winship has been indefatigable in explaining why using the Consumer Price Index (specifically a measure called "CPI-U") as the gauge of inflation is a mistake, and how it warps our understanding of economic trends. It overestimates housing inflation before 1983, and ignores how consumer behavior responds when prices change.

Since inflation compounds, small errors each year add up to major changes over decades. Use a better measure of inflation, one based on personal-consumption expenditures, and the average wage rose by 21 percent from 1973 to 2018. (Average compensation must have risen more.)

The data on median family income also show a reassuring amount of growth. The family in the middle of the pack in 2015 made 45 percent more, with the right inflation adjustment, than its counterpart in 1970.

But the same numbers may also explain some of the public's dissatisfaction with the economy. Median family income grew by a spectacular 58 percent in the 15 years from 1955 to 1970, then grew another 11 percent from 1970 to 1985, and 24 percent from 1985 to 2000. But the median family income of 2014 was slightly *lower* than it was in 2000.

What happened is that after the turn of the millennium we went through an extended period of slow growth punctuated by one mild and one severe recession. Median family income dropped more than 7 percent from 2007 through 2011, the sharpest decline since this data series started in 1953. It did not recover completely until 2015.

We have had a few good years since then. But it is not surprising that during the last two decades many Americans came to feel that their economic circumstances were stagnant and insecure. It is not surprising, either, that many of them have the sense that things used to be better—or that a generation of young people who started their work lives in a slow-growth economy tend not to have positive attitudes toward capitalism.

Instead of five decades of economic stagnation, we have had two decades of weak growth. That record does not suggest that the pro-market policies of the 1980s and 1990s were fundamentally mistaken. It suggests, rather, that we have discrete problems that deserve to be tackled.

High on the list of needed changes should be a reform of our monetary regime. It failed badly over the last dozen years. In 2008, excessive fear of inflation led the Federal Reserve to signal that it was going to tighten monetary policy even as the economy was sinking into a recession. It kept monetary conditions too tight after the crisis hit, too, for example by encouraging banks to hold additional reserves. These policies made the recession more severe and the recovery weaker. That these failures are not more widely appreciated is symptomatic of the misguided thinking that continues to govern monetary policy.

Reforms should be undertaken in other areas, too. Our higher-education system is not working for most young people. Our immense health sector includes immense inefficiency. Regions of the country with high economic growth have imposed regulations that make it prohibitively expensive for less fortunately situated Americans to move there.

So we are called to be ambitious, but not revolutionary. Capitalism does not need to be overthrown or even rethought. Rather, the principles that make markets work need to be applied to some areas where they have not been present. Our economic system does not need dismantling. But it does require invigoration.

# SWEDEN IS CAPITALIST

## It thought better of its experiment with bossy government

**BY DEIRDRE NANSEN MCCLOSKEY**

FROM the left, Sweden is the Swedish Way, hailed since the 1950s as our own best future in breathless articles among the girdle ads in *The New York Times Magazine*. From the right, it's the Road to Serfdom, which That Man in the White House was wont to lead us down.

I'm here to tell you that both are wrong. I've been over into the present, and Sweden's real per capita GDP is, in terms of purchasing power, roughly what your typical rich country earns these days. It's below that of the workaholic U.S., and—irritatingly to the Swedes, who view themselves as the natural leaders of Scandinavia and make jokes about the idiotic Norwegians—it's well below that of oil-rich Norway. But if Sweden were actually in the grip of a Communist-style socialism, as the Right fears and the Left desires, its income per head would not now, as it does, *exceed* by a little Germany's and Japan's and Britain's. It would be more like North Korea's, or Venezuela's. Around 1850, it was in fact at such levels, before an enthusiasm for bourgeois liberty and dignity took hold.

Sweden in fact is pretty much as "capitalistic" as is the United States. It's Minnesota writ large. Not writ all that large, actually, with merely 9.3 million people, many of them now foreign-born, compared with the 5.3 million Minnesotans, 10 percent of Swedish descent. Like the Land of 10,000 Lakes, Sweden is a place of private ownership and thrusting inventors, Swedish bachelor farmers and pretty generous social provision, pretty good schools (with vouchers) and terrible weather.

If "socialism" means government ownership of the means of production, which is the classic definition, Sweden never qualified. When little Sweden's economists were second in academic standing only to big Britain's, in the early 20th century, they were "liberal" in the European sense: free-traders opposed to central planning and governmental ownership. None of Sweden's manufacturing or extractive industries has ever been socialized, this in contrast, for example, to the experiment after 1946 in the world's first innovative economy, when the Labour party's Clause IV nationalized the Bank of England, coal, inland transport, gas, steel, health services, and much else. Sweden never followed even the more modest example of America's temporary nationalization of railways during the First World War. Sweden's Systembolaget, the state liquor store, was sold off in 2008, as it has not yet been in all the U.S. Apoteket, the maddeningly inefficient Swedish-government drug-store monopoly, was privatized, too, praise the Lord.

But these are small potatoes. The big potatoes in Sweden are owned by reclusive millionaires worthy of Newport, R.I., or Rancho Santa Fe, Calif. Consult Stieg Larsson and *The Girl with the Dragon Tattoo*. When Saab Autos began its descent into bankruptcy, no Swede suggested that the government give the company billions on the security of its worthless stock. When Volvo became a Chinese company, no Swede objected. Compare the determination of the Bush and Obama administrations in proudly capitalist America to socialize General Motors and Chrysler—Chrysler for the second time. Or compare the plans on the left of the Democratic party to solve any problem by expanding the government instead of solving the problem, such as monopoly in the provision of U.S. health care. "In many fields," noted a Swedish diplomat, "we have more private ownership compared to other European countries, and to America. About 80 percent of all new schools are privately run, as are the railroads and the subway system." Compare Amtrak, with eight stops in West Virginia, compliments of Senator Robert Byrd.

Anyway, the word "capitalism" doesn't capture what is special about an innovative economy such as that of Sweden or the U.S. Capital isn't the point. People have saved and invested, bought low and sold high, since Abram pulled off the property deal with the Lord. We need a better word for what happened since 1800 in the West, and now increasingly the rest. The worst enemies of liberty popularized "capitalism" in the late 19th century. We shouldn't let them go on setting the intellectual agenda.

Scientifically speaking, the C-word draws undue attention to the financial sector. Worse, it embodies a mistaken theory, still popular among some economists, right and left, that capital accumulation is what made us rich. What actually made American and Swedish and Japanese people rich was innovation, that is, invention-carried-out, "exchange-tested betterment," you might say, or even "innovism." For instance, to speak only of new ways of doing (the modern world was also made by new ways of speaking): the screw propeller in steamships, the blowtorch, the safety match, the improved zipper, Nobel's dynamite, the adjustable wrench, the pacemaker, dialysis, ultrasound, IKEA furniture, the three-point safety belt, the precision ball-bearing in, for example, automobiles ("Volvo" means in Latin "I roll," and honors the company's spinoff in the 1920s from Svenska Kullagerfabriken, SKF, still the leading ball-bearing maker in the world). All these were betterments tested by exchange in tiny Sweden, right up to the present.

A non-technical definition of "socialism" would be "bossy and obstructive and high-handed government." Sweden certainly has a good deal of that, inspired for example by the eugenicists Gunnar and Alva Myrdal in the 1930s. Sweden, with other Protestant countries, led the world in compulsory sterilization and persecution of gays into the 1970s. It's an example of the way the Swedes go along with their government too much, sometimes because they assume too easily that whatever is widely agreed must be right. An old Swedish woman left her worn-out frying pan in a trash container for metal *packages*. She was arrested for committing a crime against the environment, freed only after trial, and fined. Nice.

Yet for bossy and obstructive and high-handed government in the Land of the Free, what about the many American states that had sterilization laws in 1956? What about the drug-war/incarceration complex, destroying black and Hispanic families and neighborhoods and denying the vote to millions of "felons"? Or the U.S. military expelling good soldiers, some of whom speak Arabic, for nearly two decades because they were openly gay—and now because they are transgendered?

Swedish-government spending, true, is very high, half again as large, measured as a share of GDP, as government spending in the U.S. If we could commission the Swedes to come over and run the American government, I'd be willing to feed the beast. Like Iowa (Minnesota a little less so), and unlike Illinois, Sweden has honest government, to which you wouldn't mind giving that extra krone, since after all a good deal of it comes back in actual services and never goes into Swiss bank accounts.

In 1960 Sweden had a normal, rich, and *capitalist* economy, having developed from the 1850s after free-market reforms from being the poorest country in Western Europe to being the fourth-richest in the world. In 1938 at Saltsjöbaden, while FDR in the U.S. was still ranting against economic royalists and terrifying the investing class, the unions and corporations in Sweden were agreeing to industrial peace under the Social Democratic regime, which gave wide latitude to the industrialists for investing in technology and earning profits. Seventy percent of working Swedes nowadays belong to a union, a greatly higher rate than in the U.S. at the height of industrial unionism. But unlike, say, the U.S., with its many decades of protecting steel production and its century of keeping sugar prices at twice the world level, Sweden let its shipbuilding industry die quickly, and if you visit factories in Sweden you are struck by how many robots work there. It's a result of export-oriented managers' facing export-conceding unions. The unions in bigger countries, less obviously dependent on foreign trade, still think that by stopping innovation they can "protect" workers.

True, Sweden—like the U.S. at the same time—had an era from 1960 to 1976 of dogmatic and union-driven extensions of the welfare state. Olof Palme said in the 1960s, "The political winds are to the left: Let us set sail." Sweden still supports able-bodied people who decide not to work very much. Some don't work at all, declaring, "I am allergic to electricity." And among working Swedes, in this healthiest of modern countries, with six-week paid vacations, absenteeism for illness is over a month a year. Such policies drove Swedish income per capita down to 17th in the world, though at the gain of eliminating much poverty.

But Sweden can't be our future in the United States, not unless we give up our beloved ethic of *Folktillfältet*, the people's opportunity, and its corollary, I've-Got-Mine. It's an ethic embodied for example in the "agency theory" that dominates modern American business schools. A non-academic version was articulated by the Tammany Hall politician George Washington Plunkitt in 1905: "There's an honest graft, and I'm an example of how it works. I might sum up the whole thing by sayin': 'I seen my opportunities and I took 'em.'" We laugh, because we are Americans, or Chicagoans, or work for Goldman Sachs.

It's a sort of socialism, come to think of it, in another key. But it ain't Swedish.

# THE CASE FOR FREE TRADE

## It is economic and moral

BY SCOTT LINCICOME

THE policy of free trade—citizens freely buying and selling goods and services across borders without government interference—is under greater attack today than it has been in decades. Despite the fact that American public support for trade and globalization is at an all-time high, politicians, pundits, and a growing cadre of wonks on both the left and the right have become increasingly hostile to the long-standing U.S. political consensus in favor of multilateral trade liberalization. This hostility, however, is mostly misguided. Although it contains certain nuggets of truth about, for example, Chinese mercantilism or onerous trade-agreement rules, the case for free trade—economic, geopolitical, and, perhaps most of all, moral—is as strong today as it was when Adam Smith wrote *The Wealth of Nations* almost 250 years ago.

Trade and globalization have provided undeniable economic benefits for the vast majority of American families, businesses, and workers. Most obvious are the consumer gains. Several recent studies have found that freer trade with China, for example, has generated, through increased competition and lower prices, hundreds of billions of dollars in U.S. consumer benefits—benefits that, according to economists Xavier Jaravel and Erick Sager, are the equivalent of giving every American "$260 of extra spending per year for the rest of their lives." Consumer gains from imports, in general tilted toward the poor and the middle class, are especially tilted toward them when it comes to goods that are made in China and sold at stores like Walmart. The magnitude of such benefits also debunks the well-worn myth that free trade is mainly about cheap T-shirts. Indeed, trade's consumer surplus is a big reason that Americans today work far fewer hours to own far better essentials than at any prior time in U.S. history.

Then there are trade's overall benefits for the economy. A 2017 Peterson Institute paper calculated the payoff to the United States from expanded trade between 1950 and 2016 to be $2.1 trillion, increasing U.S. GDP per capita and per household by around $7,000 and $18,000—with benefits, again, disproportionately accruing to households in the bottom income decile. The U.S. International Trade Commission, moreover, found in 2016 that U.S. bilateral and regional trade agreements such as NAFTA generated small but significant annual increases in GDP, as well as in employment and real wages among highly skilled and less skilled American workers. As the American Enterprise Institute's Michael Strain has noted, trade-skeptical populists who downplay this impressive macroeconomic boost ignore that, as our current economic moment attests, a small bit of extra GDP growth can mean big things for lower-wage, lower-skill workers in terms of employment and possible government assistance.

Trade and globalization also support American companies and workers, even in manufacturing. The Commerce Department, for example, has estimated that almost 11 million jobs depended on exports of U.S. goods and services in 2016, and foreign direct investment in the United States—the necessary flip side of our oft-maligned trade deficit—supported millions more. Meanwhile, American companies that adapt and thrive in today's economy most often do so by making use of imports and global supply chains. The San Francisco Fed, for instance, recently estimated that almost half of U.S. imports are intermediate products purchased by American manufacturers to make globally competitive finished goods; the country's biggest exporters, therefore, are also its biggest importers. Numerous other studies have found that the vast majority of the value of an American company's assembled-abroad product (such as an iPhone, assembled in China) accrues to the U.S. company, including its workers and shareholders—not to the place of final assembly (despite what a gross bilateral trade balance, which attributes an import's full cost to its final export source, might say).

These supply chains not only deliver modern marvels at amazing prices but also allow American companies and workers to focus on our high-value comparative advantages, such as professional services and advanced manufacturing, and leave the lower-value stuff to other countries and workers who lack such skills. Imports, the San Francisco Fed study found, also support millions of other American jobs in transportation, logistics, and wholesale and retail trade—indeed, almost half of all U.S. consumption dollars spent on items not "made in the USA" go to these Americans, not to foreigners.

Finally, there are the immense, unseen benefits of import competition on American economic dynamism (a market's rate of change and innovation) and living standards. "When we find ways to get more from less, that means more resources available to expand opportunities elsewhere in the economy," George Mason's Russ Roberts recently noted. "That expansion is unseen. . . . But it's hugely important." Whether this creative destruction comes from trade or technology is irrelevant: The outcome is not just cheaper stuff but better (and once unimaginable) stuff, better jobs, better companies, and better lives. And it can occur only by letting consumers and their capital seek more-productive ends.

This is why the alternative to freer trade, taken to its extreme, is not $2,000 iPhones; it's no iPhones at all.

Protectionism, meanwhile, has repeatedly proven a costly failure. When researchers at the International Monetary Fund recently examined tariff increases in 151 different countries between 1963 and 2014, they found that correlated with such policies were significant declines in domestic output and productivity, more unemployment, and higher inequality. The United States is not immune to these harmful forces: Two new studies, from economists with the National Bureau of Economic Research, have found that the economic pain from Trump's 2018 tariffs fell entirely on American consumers (companies and individuals). My 2017 survey of the academic literature on over a century of U.S. protectionism pre-Trump showed that, with very few exceptions, it imposed immense economic costs on American consumers, workers, and companies (more than $600,000 per year for every U.S. job created) while also failing to open foreign markets or resuscitate protected American firms and workers over the longer term. In case after case, the jobs still disappeared, and the companies either went bankrupt or came back to the government for more help. And it's happening again: Though American steel consumers are paying much higher prices than their global competitors, U.S. steel-industry stocks lag far behind the S&P 500 index. For these and related reasons, economists of the Left, Right, and center continue to oppose tariffs overwhelmingly (93 percent of a recent IGM Economic Experts Panel of dozens of top economists, to be exact), and they support freer trade and globalization.

In addition to generating economic benefits, trade has also long been a pillar of national and global security. As the Brookings Institution's Robert Kagan noted in a *Washington Post* op-ed in 2018, the multilateral trading system arose not from a desire for global economic growth or to empower global consumers but from a fear of another global war. And this system, for all its fits and starts, met that aim reasonably well for more than seven decades. Since the end of World War II, Kagan wrote, the global trading system helped prevent "the slightest danger that economic competition would spill over into geopolitical competition"—"one of the great historical anomalies" of our time. The World Trade Organization has provided an impressively effective venue for the resolution of bilateral trade disputes as well as a key way—primarily through the accession process and its numerous obligations—for developing countries to undertake painful internal reforms as the "price" of joining the WTO, reforms that otherwise might have been too politically difficult. (Even China undertook such reforms, and its post-accession backsliding is far more a failure of WTO members' enforcement than of the accession commitments themselves.) The WTO system certainly isn't perfect, but it's still far preferable to the piecemeal system of power politics, uncertainty, and outright war that preceded it. Indeed, the United States' recent shift back toward this old system of bilateral deals and unilateral enforcement is already causing anxiety around the world, even for some of our closest allies, such as Japan and the U.K.

Finally, removing U.S. restrictions on Americans' consumption of foreign goods, services, and capital is not merely an economic and geopolitical decision but also a moral one. Whether intended or not, trade liberalization has removed stark inequities in the previous, protectionist U.S. system—inequities that typically originated in a proverbial smoke-filled room full of lobbyists and elite policymakers. Protectionism invisibly propped up certain industries and workers at most Americans' expense and generated the aforementioned economic and geopolitical problems.

Indeed, we are witnessing again today just how protectionism breeds elite cronyism and political dysfunction and hurts far more Americans than it helps. Former "big steel" lawyers and executives, now in the Trump administration, dole out tariff protection to their former colleagues who lobbied for it; those well-connected colleagues, in turn, get to decide the fate of their American customers' requests for steel-tariff relief, even though the steel-consuming customers are a far larger share of the U.S. economy and work force than is the steel industry. And that's just the steel tariffs. Is it any wonder that trade-related lobbying expenditures over the past two years have skyrocketed? Those on the left who aim to "get money out of politics" and those on the right who talk of "draining the swamp" reveal the weakness of such commitments when they turn a blind eye to the corruption directly resulting from the protectionist policies they support.

Why should certain American industries and workers have a moral claim to government protection? Why should government prioritize those workers' living standards above their fellow citizens'? American footwear workers, for example, have long benefited from a government policy dating back to the Smoot-Hawley Tariff Act of 1930 that protects their jobs through hidden restrictions on the commerce of other Americans—restrictions that force everyone, including the poor, to subsidize footwear jobs by paying more for their shoes. Perhaps, if the taxes were repealed and Americans could buy shoes from whomever they wished, the nation would owe affected workers welfare or job training. But the workers are not owed the protection itself, and its removal is not an immoral act. It is the right thing to do, and the broader economic and geopolitical gains are just gravy.

The morality of trade does not stop at the water's edge, either: The lowering of U.S. trade barriers, along with American leadership in creating agreements and institutions such as the WTO, has produced immeasurable benefits for the world's poorest people. As the World Bank noted in its *Report on the Role of Trade in Ending Poverty*, since 1990, "a dramatic increase in developing-country participation in trade has coincided with an equally sharp decline in extreme poverty worldwide," and the number of people living in extreme poverty has collapsed. Trade has also "helped increase the number and quality of jobs in developing countries, stimulated economic growth, and driven productivity increases."

A new report from the International Labor Organization provides jaw-dropping stats in this regard: Between 1993 and 2018, the share of individuals in low- and middle-income countries working in extreme poverty fell from almost 42 percent to less than 10 percent—a decline of around 600 million people. Most moved from subsistence farming to formal wage or salary work, providing themselves with first-time access to health care and other benefits. And, contrary to popular belief, the job creation in developing countries did not happen primarily in "sweatshop" manufacturing: The share of industrial workers in low- and middle-income countries almost did not change between 1991 and 2018, with job growth instead coming from sectors such as construction and retail trade; between 1999 and 2017, inflation-adjusted real wages in these countries tripled. Child labor is also disappearing: The overall number of child workers (ages five to 17) decreased by approximately 94 million between 2000 and 2016 (from 246 million to 152 million) and is projected to decline by tens of millions more by 2025. These improvements have been especially strong among women and girls, who in many countries faced truly horrible social conditions (hunger, arranged marriages, etc.) before these new jobs existed.

Trade liberalization contributes to all of this.

Free trade is certainly not costless, and experts have surely miscalculated projected trade flows and their effects on certain labor markets. But the problems that some Americans face as a result of free trade do not outweigh its tremendous overall benefits for the country and the world. And the downsides of free trade cannot obscure either its fundamental morality or the proven pain and inefficacy of the lone alternative, protectionism. They also cannot change the fact that much of today's globalization is driven not by "trade deals" or other top-down policy choices but by seismic technological shifts, such as the Internet and shipping containers; that the post-war world, of which large portions were recovering from war or descending into Communism, was a unique situation for American manufacturing workers; that, historically, technology has been responsible for eliminating most low- and middle-skill manufacturing jobs in America, and that it would eventually have consumed the others, too; and, finally, that the problems of small towns in "flyover" country may be, as Tim Carney documents in his new book *Alienated America*, due more to the collapse of cultural institutions such as marriage, church, and civic life than to any economic forces.

These challenges are some of the hardest of our time, and the solutions are neither clear nor easy. But a rejection of freer trade and an embrace of protectionism would only make things worse.

# 'CHINESE CAPITALISM' IS AN OXYMORON

## What Beijing has established is not a market economy

**BY ROBERT ATKINSON**

IN his classic 1967 book *Modern–of Public and Private Power*, Andrew Shonfield tried to make sense of the distinctly different flavors of capitalism that evolved in the post-war era: the German model, where large banks played a key role in allocating investment; the Italian model of public–private ownership of key industries; the French model of indicative planning; the Japanese model of state-led industrial policy; and the American and British models of largely free-market, laissez-faire capitalism, albeit leavened with a growing social-welfare state.

He concluded that, notwithstanding their differences, advanced capitalist economies share basic convictions, including that private capital should be at the center of economic activity, that market-based transactions are the key to prosperity, and that private property should be protected. To be sure, the Left and the Right fight over how to achieve the proper balance of these factors—fights that appear to be intensifying—but most agree on the core principles. In short, any differences between capitalist nations are of degree, not of kind.

This has long led defenders of capitalism to suffer from a certain level of hubris: Isn't it obvious that the capitalist cookbook is the best? One need only look back at the failed Communist experiment in the Soviet Union for proof. Indeed, as Francis Fukuyama told us in *The End of History*, "the triumph of the West" included a triumph of market-based capitalism.

But these days, as we struggle to figure out the puzzle that is China, things aren't so clear. To be sure, China, propelled by private firms, has transformed itself from a Communist basket case where the masses wore Mao suits into the world's second-largest economy. Because China is less Communist than it once was, many simply assume it has become capitalist. Wall Street financier Steven Rattner argues that "despite its Communist heritage," China "understands the benefits of incorporating a robust free-enterprise element." Nobel laureate Ronald Coase and his co-author Ning Wang proclaim that China has "embraced capitalism," citing, in part, the fact that Adam Smith's book *The Theory of Moral Sentiments* has more than a dozen Chinese translations.

But just because China has many private companies, allows Communist-Party member Jack Ma to become a billionaire as head of Alibaba Group, and translates capitalist classics into Mandarin doesn't mean it's capitalist. The fact that few describe the Chinese economic system without putting a modifier in front of the term "capitalism"—"authoritarian," "state," "predatory," "Communist," etc.—should tell us something. As should the fact that the Chinese Communist Party, which follows the "guidance of Marxism-Leninism," calls for a socialist market economy. The reality is that the differences between the Chinese and Western variants of capitalism are more of kind than of degree.

China is a hybrid economy in which the state uses an array of tools for Communist-Party ends. To start with, China has more than 150,000 state-owned enterprises, accounting for 40 percent of industrial assets. However, Chinese state capitalism is not just, or even principally, about the number and size of such enterprises; it's about the central role the Chinese Communist Party (CCP) plays in virtually all aspects of economic life. In fact, CCP officials are part of many Chinese companies "to make sure the company follows the law."

China takes great pains to paint its party-directed efforts in the most genial light. Indeed, when you feel compelled to publish an English-language cartoon on Twitter touting how your 13th Five-Year Plan is a fun, progressive activity, your propaganda department is earning its yuan. (Interestingly enough, while the Chinese government is happy to put its propaganda on Twitter, it blocks access to Twitter in China.) Indeed, the party takes great effort to make its central planning sound nothing like a cold, sterile, Stalinist enterprise but rather a jubilant, bottom-up exercise developed by cherubic-faced workers and wise intelligentsia. Who actually makes the plans? Not a clutch of dour bureaucrats in Beijing. Rather, the cartoon jingle explains, "There's government ministers and think-tank minds, and party leadership contributing finds. There's doctors, bankers, and farmers too, and even engineers who deal with poo." Oh, how fun.

No Twitter video can disguise the fact that, at its heart, Chinese state capitalism is a system in which the purpose of firms—private and public—is to fulfill the goals of the

Communist Party. And the CCP uses an array of tools to obtain that alignment: hard and soft power; carrots and sticks. One tool is turning a blind eye to, and in many cases actively instigating, intellectual-property theft from foreign organizations. Another is requiring most foreign firms to enter into joint ventures with Chinese firms as a condition of market access—an arrangement the Chinese call "exchanging market for technology." On top of that, central and provincial governments provide hundreds of billions of dollars' worth of subsidies to China's domestic champions in industries that range from steel and auto parts to jet aircraft and semiconductors.

The government also intervenes in currency markets, as it has done over the past year in response to the Trump administration's imposition of 10 percent tariffs on a wide array of Chinese imports: It engineered a counterbalancing 10 percent decline in the value of the yuan relative to the dollar. Underlying all this is the almost complete absence of a rule of law to constrain party officials. The courts are part of the state apparatus, and few administrative agencies are transparent in their regulations.

One reason for confusion in the West about the Chinese economic system is that many see capitalism simply as a system built on private ownership of property. But capitalism is more than that. It is a system in which those property owners have considerable—albeit not unlimited—freedom to pursue their goals without influence from the state. By this standard, China's is far from a capitalist economy.

The last time two competing and incompatible economic systems faced each other, each side erected firewalls. Beyond the occasional sale of a few consumer items, such as Pepsi, in Russia, there was very little trade or investment between First World market-based nations and Second World Communist nations. But by 2001, just ten years after the fall of the Soviet Union, people thought Communism was a 20th-century relic. It was against that backdrop that China not only was allowed to join the World Trade Organization (WTO) but was warmly embraced, amid high hopes that its accession would lead it to take the final steps necessary to become a truly market-based economy. Incoming WTO chairman Supachai Panitchpakdi summarized the view of most at the time when he wrote that joining would signal "China's willingness to play by international trade rules and to bring its often opaque and cumbersome governmental apparatus into harmony with a world order that demands clarity and fairness."

Needless to say, as even the most ardent defenders of China's WTO accession now acknowledge, that did not happen. In fact, as the Information Technology and Innovation Foundation and other groups have shown, there is a yawning gap between China's WTO commitments and its actual trade and economic practices. The result is that in a deeply integrated global economy, two very different systems now coexist.

That coexistence has proven highly damaging to global innovation and economic growth. To see why, imagine that the Department of Justice randomly assigns half of U.S. corporations to be A-corps and half to be B-corps. For A-corps, nothing changes. But B-corps now enjoy special privileges and rules. They are exempt from laws governing intellectual-property theft. They receive more-favorable tax incentives.

They are recipients of sizable subsidies, including some to buy their A-corp rivals. They are able to enlist the DOJ to win capricious legal claims against A-corp rivals.

The result of such an experiment would be dire: The best, most innovative A-corp firms would lose market share; A-corps would be loath to invest in research and development, given that B-corp rivals would be able to purloin it; and there would be massive waste as inefficient B-corp firms expanded more than market forces required. Now extrapolate that to the global economy and you get a sense of the harms the Chinese system has imposed on capitalist economies.

Western capitalist economies now face three strategic choices. The first is to muddle through, hoping that China shoots itself in the foot and that the overall damage to it and the global economy is not too great. The second is to move in the direction of the Cold War–era, two-economies system. Indeed, we are potentially seeing the beginning of that, in part with the growing movement by capitalist economies to ban sales of Huawei telecommunications equipment. The third is for Western capitalist democracies, presumably under U.S. leadership, to band together, press China to reform, and establish global trade rules with real teeth. Choice three is clearly the best for the world. Let's hope President Trump, and whoever succeeds him, selects it. And let's stop pretending that what exists in China is capitalism.

# MICHAEL NOVAK NOW

## The Spirit of Democratic Capitalism grounds markets in the Judeo-Christian tradition

BY SAMUEL GREGG

In my last conversation with Michael Novak, shortly before his death in 2017, he expressed his regret that socialism was undergoing a revival in America. "Well," Novak said wearily, "I guess you're going to have to re-explain—yet again—all the problems with socialism. Apparently, someone has to do it [pause] every [pause] single [pause] generation."

Novak was a natural optimist. Yet he knew that once people become enamored of whatever is being called "socialism" at any given time, changing their views becomes extremely difficult. In the mid 1960s, Novak saw most of his academic contemporaries embrace economic positions far to the left of what their parents had endorsed when voting for Franklin Roosevelt in the 1930s.

Novak himself wandered down that path. He once confessed that as a young man he had been "moved by the socialism of Charles Péguy, the French Catholic poet who saw in socialism not so much a doctrine as a way of life."

That Novak was once "one of them" is one reason I'd suggest to the 51 percent of Americans aged 18 to 29 who, according to a 2018 Gallup poll, favor socialism that they read Novak's 1982 classic *The Spirit of Democratic Capitalism*. That's especially true if they are of Jewish or Christian faith. Yes, some of the book is dated. But its insights into socialism and capitalism are as powerful as they were 37 years ago.

Part Two of the book, "The Twilight of Socialism," is particularly instructive. Here Novak detailed the economic problems bedeviling socialism, whether of the command-economy type or contemporary social democracy. Novak never claimed that economics should be decisive in political choices. But he did think that the basic insights into reality provided by economics—the workings of incentives and self-interest, comparative advantage, trade-offs, the necessity of free prices as carriers of information, attentiveness to the known side effects of particular choices, etc.—should no more be ignored than any other empirically validated observation arising from the social sciences.

The lessons of economics, however, weren't the primary point of departure for Novak's critique of socialism. He genuinely wanted to understand why people embrace socialism, and he concluded that it wasn't simply economic ignorance.

By the early 1980s, Novak argued, socialism had become less about practical economic programs than about (1) certain ideals regarding equality and poverty and (2) deep hostility to capitalism per se. The single-minded pursuit of these beliefs, combined with the tendency to view capitalism in almost demonic terms, meant that socialism assumed the form of what Novak called a "political religion." This, he believed, was what made socialism erroneous—and very dangerous.

Being a political faith, socialism could never fulfill the expectations associated with true religion. But its ersatz religious nature meant that socialism's economic and political failures would inevitably generate a very particular type of fury.

Socialism's record of failure, Novak pointed out, was clear. Instead of growing wealth across society, it gradually impoverished all. Far from producing greater equality, it facilitated its own inequities, the most glaring being those between the planners and everyone else.

Faced with these disappointments, socialism-as-a-faith needed scapegoats to affirm its own righteousness and that of its practitioners. Such culprits have included businessmen, foreigners, America, and the Jews. The anti-Semitic rantings of Maduro-regime officials in Venezuela are no more incidental to "21st-Century Socialism" than the "anti-Zionist" campaigns pursued in Eastern European Communist states in the late 1960s were to those regimes.

These insights, I'd suggest, highlight a point underscored by Novak that might encourage today's socialists to reconsider their animus against capitalism.

Throughout *The Spirit of Democratic Capitalism*, Novak was relentless in stressing that any serious theory of political economy must pay attention to the human condition. Humans are good yet capable of evil. Our reason is powerful but not all-powerful. Men are not angels, but neither are they beasts. The genius of market economies, Novak held, is that they recognize humanity's capacities and limitations and help direct them to the realization of some important goods.

This argument first achieved mature form during the Scottish Enlightenment. Novak, however, had a way of explaining it to late-20th-century audiences and investing it with distinctly American experiences.

Commercial republics such as America, Novak argued, had shown how allowing people to pursue their self-interest within a particular political and legal context indirectly helped to establish important material and political conditions of the common good. What's more, they showed that you didn't need a planner with pretensions to omnipotence—the "man of system" of whom Adam Smith spoke—to engineer such outcomes.

But while Novak's political economy was partly derived from a hard-headed assessment of human nature, he was as focused on ideals as any dedicated socialist. His vision was one of a market economy enmeshed in a political system that took equity and freedom seriously, with everything ultimately grounded in the particular moral culture derived from the best of Jewish and Christian thought and practice.

Novak was always a culture-first man, long before Rod Dreher proposed his "Benedict option" of the formation of monastic-like communities dedicated to Christian living in a secularizing world. As much as he admired the great explanatory power of free-market economics, particularly Friedrich von Hayek's version, Novak understood that the preservation of freedom and justice depends less upon economics than it does on the vision of man at the heart of any culture.

Here Novak's ideas about morality and markets were close to those of the German economist, devout Christian, and intellectual architect of West Germany's market-driven economic miracle, Wilhelm Röpke. Both Röpke and Novak understood the civilizational imperative of grounding markets in a particular culture that shapes people's choices towards non-libertine ends.

This was why Novak would have pushed back against some contemporary conservatives' lazy association of free markets with ethical hedonism or my-body-is-my-property arguments. He certainly recognized that some free-market advocates do think in such terms. Novak, however, held that you can have a dynamic market *and* a culture in which millions can pursue a plurality of different but compatible goods rooted in the truth about man. To be sure, Novak acknowledged that there would always be tensions. That, however, is the price of giving people the space to pursue the higher freedom to which reason and the Jewish and Christian faiths point as the telos of liberty.

Of course, there are many contemporary economic, cultural, and political issues that Novak didn't address. The cronyism infecting places such as New York City, Washington, D.C., and Chicago isn't given much attention in his writings. Nor did Novak anticipate the extent to which corporate America would embrace an infantile leftism to prove how "woke" it is.

I've no doubt, however, that Novak would have had ready responses to these problems. He would have pointed out, for instance, that the temptation for business to wander down the crony path grows whenever the state starts assuming a larger role in the economy. This wasn't simply because Novak knew his Adam Smith, including the Scot's attention to the phenomenon of privilege-seeking businesses' and privilege-dispensing legislators' enriching each other at everyone else's expense. Novak also took the biblical idea of sin very seriously—far more seriously, I think, than some of capitalism's contemporary religious critics. This led Novak to a deep realism about humans and power.

Politics was important to Novak. It mattered, he believed, who held political power. Nor was he a knee-jerk anti-government type. But politicians, Novak knew, were as affected by sin as anyone else. And sins such as pride often encouraged hubris about what governments could do. The results were often disastrous.

This didn't mean that Novak thought liberty and markets would eventually take care of everything. He didn't. Many of the social dysfunctionalities that worry socialism's advocates and capitalism's critics don't have market solutions because, Novak understood, their causes often have little to do with economics. Nor, however, did he think that politics always provided answers.

Novak never tired of observing that two of his heroes, Alexis de Tocqueville and Jacques Maritain, had highlighted America's long history of civil-society-first solutions to social challenges. This, Novak believed, had enabled much of America to avoid some of the mistakes associated with the state-first policies pursued by the European Left and Right. America's approach might be "messier," yet Novak was convinced it was more effective than the top-down approaches that enamor intellectuals.

Herein, I'd argue, lies Novak's ultimate importance for America's contemporary economic debates. Capitalism isn't the kingdom of heaven. Then again, Novak never claimed it was. He reminds us, however, that some humility can help us to see the underlying errors of an economic system that has produced mass death or, in its milder forms, the slow bureaucratization of life that is evident in much of Western Europe. As Novak often said, hell is what happens when you pursue heaven-on-earth. That's a truth that today's socialists and critics of capitalism should—assuming they're interested in doing more than just signaling their virtue—really take to heart.

# THE LOST GENERATIONS?

## Don't write off Millennials and Gen Z

**BY JIMMY QUINN**

THE prognosis was dark, the response fast and furious. "People our age have never experienced American prosperity in our adult lives—which is why so many millennials are embracing Democratic socialism," wrote journalist Charlotte Alter, sharing her *Time* profile of Alexandria Ocasio-Cortez on Twitter. Her reformulation of the congresswoman's words quickly became a flashpoint online.

Point: The economy's booming. Millennials are lazy, vain things that pay up for Instagrammable experiences and anything avocado. They live in their parents' basements because they can't be bothered to pay rent, or a mortgage. Counterpoint (offered by AOC and crew): Millennials are destitute because they've been screwed by the Boomers. They're strangled by the high cost of education and health care, and by an uneven economic recovery. Business is roaring, but only a select few enjoy its fruits.

Which do you think resonates more with young Americans? Defenders of free markets could win this debate on the merits. Unemployment is down, and GDP growth last year was around 3 percent, the precise number depending on which measure you prefer to use. Yet anyone paying attention knows that Millennials aren't buying it. Their skepticism of capitalism is now common knowledge.

At least partly because of this, some business leaders, such as Bridgewater's Ray Dalio, are hedging their bets. Absent significant reforms to capitalism, "some form of revolution" might be around the corner. Is that wrong? A seemingly endless series of polls would appear to show growing support for socialism (and declining support for capitalism) among the Millennial generation and the similarly liberal college students and teenagers who compose Generation Z. In 2020, these two cohorts will account for 37 percent of the voting-age population.

However, polls that suggest growing Millennial support for socialism seem to generate more alarm than the truth would warrant. Take, for instance, an *Axios* survey that found in January that 61 percent of 18- to 24-year-olds and 51 percent of 25- to 34-year-olds had a positive reaction to socialism. While this result indicates the dissipation of a taboo on the use of that label, 58 percent of both cohorts also viewed capitalism in a favorable light. Along similar lines, an *Axios*/Harris Survey in February showed that 49.6 percent of Millennials and Gen Zers would prefer to live in a socialist country—much lower than the 73.2 percent and the 67.1 percent, who, respectively, support universal health care and free college tuition.

This presents a mixed bag. There is stronger support for expanding government programs than for "socialism," which might just be another buzzword for progressive policies anyway. And as striking as high levels of support for those policies may be, it's not unreasonable to predict that survey questions framed in terms of their cost could significantly lower those numbers. Still, the general Millennial preference for these proposals cannot just be wished away.

The conservative response has largely been to say something about Venezuela or the Soviet Union. Although this is, again, correct on the merits, anyone who has talked socialism with a left-wing college student knows to expect a familiar rejoinder: Venezuela and the USSR don't represent *true* socialism, and instead we should look to Sweden and Denmark. The more daring might even counter that Stalinism was bad but capitalism has its own body count, as author Mike Davis claimed in a *Jacobin* interview last October.

So if socialism to Millennials is Denmark, not Venezuela, "the right answer is not that Denmark is hell—it is not hell—but the right answer is that in fact for Denmark to work, the whole original socialist model had to be reformed in a way that empowered entrepreneurship," argued the economist Edward Glaeser during a lecture last year. To boot, these Millennials, he said, are awfully confident that we'd resemble Sweden more than we would Greece. Disabusing them of these misconceptions is a logical first step.

But it would be a mistake to ignore the general Millennial dissatisfaction with current economic conditions. As Michael Hobbes has noted at *HuffPost*, studies link higher unemployment with notably lower starting salaries; members of the class of 2009 could expect to earn close to $60,000 less over ten years than those who graduated before the financial crisis. Ocasio-Cortez, Boston University '11, speaks for the generation that ventured into the job market during the recession. Recovery be damned, that leaves an impression near impossible to erase from the political consciousness of that generation, which maybe explains the nearly tenfold increase in membership that the Democratic Socialists of America have enjoyed over the past three years.

Interestingly, dissatisfaction with the status quo hasn't benefited the DSA only; it's also put wind in the sails of Millennial advocates of urban development. *CityLab* called 2018 "the Year of the YIMBY," referring to pro-development activists who push their local officials to approve zoning deregulation in hopes of increasing the supply of housing and therefore lowering rents. Minneapolis became the movement's first success when its city council voted to eliminate single-family zoning in December. Progressive supporters touted the plan's potential to fight racism, climate change, and economic inequality—but that shouldn't obscure a clear victory for free markets.

The national conversation about Millennials and capitalism surrounds the big-ticket items that we hear about all the time. However, Millennials also care strongly about pocketbook expenses and everyday conveniences, something that proponents of capitalism would be well advised to exploit. If Amazon stifles competition and mistreats its workers, you wouldn't know it based on Gen Z and Millennial spending habits. According to one survey, 77 percent of 18- to 34-year-olds would give up alcohol if they had to choose between that and an Amazon subscription. A litany of scandals appears incapable of putting an end to Uber's popularity with Millennials. And although teens might describe the owners of Chick-fil-A as homophobic, the fast-food chain toppled Starbucks as their favorite restaurant across all levels of income last year.

The disconnect between that urban-Millennial libertarian impulse and the generation's leftist inclinations offers a tantalizing opportunity. Leaders willing to go to bat for the gig economy might reap political rewards. That said, Gen Z might be even more socially progressive than the Millennials. Gen Zers show up at the march, shift consumer preferences to match their values (even if that's not always true), and view politics in terms of justice. To them, for instance, climate change isn't just an existential threat to the planet; it's also a source of racial and economic inequality.

The Green New Deal pledges—among *many* other things—a new social contract to roll back these injustices. It also throws into relief the trade-off between free markets, on the one hand, and significant government action to restrict carbon emissions in the United States, on the other. Generation Z might get on board with the latter option, perhaps without really considering the alternatives. And that is in part because few alternatives existed until Republican members of Congress had to start rebutting arguments for the GND, even as young voters across both parties were significantly more likely than older ones to consider climate change a problem. Failure on the right to coalesce around market-friendly solutions—such as a version of Lamar Alexander's "New Manhattan Project" or even the carbon-dividends plan endorsed by thousands of economists—might just push young voters toward the GND by default.

More than political necessity, though, the moral case for capitalism must take center stage. Teenagers coming of age in today's political climate know only an ascendant socialist Left and a conservative movement increasingly influenced by skeptics of free markets, such as Tucker Carlson, who see many of capitalism's proponents as obsequious worshipers of free markets. It has become clear that capitalism needs defenders from the left and the right, especially given that three in ten Republican 18- to 24-year-olds hold a positive view of socialism. The critics provide food for thought and ideas for reform. But what remains practically ignored in today's politics is the most essential argument of all, that free-market capitalism has drastically improved the standard of living, especially for the poor.

And so, even as Millennials see themselves rowing against the current with Gatsbyesque futility, they might still be receptive to a message that favors capitalism. Gen Z, maybe more so. An episode from another Fitzgerald novel, *This Side of Paradise*, shows why. Toward the end of the book, disaffected protagonist Amory Blaine expounds on the virtues of socialism during a brief car-ride-turned-debate with a capitalist. Probed about the sincerity of his views, he admits, "Until I talked to you I hadn't thought seriously about it. I wasn't sure of half of what I said."

Responding again to his interlocutor, he continues, "I simply state that I'm a product of a versatile mind in a restless generation—every reason to throw my mind and pen in with the radicals."

The argument for capitalism is not lost as long as young voters are still forming their views. They can be persuaded, but not if they are written off.

# IN DEFENSE OF CAPITAL MARKETS

## Though no defense is needed

**BY DAVID L. BAHNSEN**

MUSTERING the courage to launch a public criticism of financiers these days doesn't exactly require the grit of Dietrich Bonhoeffer or the bravery of a Navy SEAL. Today, the very terms "hedge funds," "private equity," "Wall Street," and "investment banker" have a pejorative connotation. Critics of finance feel no need to distinguish between good actors and bad actors, and in fact the criticisms are hardly ever personalized; it is the capital markets themselves that have become unwelcome in our society, not just David Solomon or Jamie Dimon.

But establishing that finance is not popular does not tell us whether the critiques are right. One could argue that there is a track record of arrogance, excess, and combustion that has lent great sympathy to the cause of anti-finance. The financial crisis hardly created this impulse—Wall Streeters were not atop popularity lists before it—but the demonization reached a new level after Dick Fuld managed Lehman Brothers into bankruptcy and Jimmy Cayne's Bear Stearns fell. The enduring conclusion that Main Street formed about

Wall Street's behavior before the financial crisis was that it had been reckless, greedy, and indifferent to the impact of its behavior as long as bonuses were paid. Adding to the crescendo of animosity, the TARP legislation carved into our consciousness the idea that the victim of the financial crisis (Main Street, in this broadly accepted narrative) was "bailing out" the perpetrator (Wall Street). If one had wanted to make finance hated for a generation, one hardly could have written a better script.

And while Wall Street (along with the NFL, the textile industry, clean energy, big oil, food and beverage, and youth soccer) has had its fair share of fat cats and disrepute, the public's antagonism toward financiers is not attributable to a few bad apples. There is a hole in the public's understanding of capital markets, and it explains the contemporary negativity about finance. So we must be very clear—there is no capitalism without capital markets.

That it is necessary to make an argument for financial markets is itself a testimony to the economic ignorance that has permeated our society. But let us state the obvious: While employment and rising wages are vital benefits of a business, they are not its objective. The objective is, rather, the delivery of a good or service to a customer who wants it. So while hampering businesses threatens jobs and wage growth, it also hampers the development and delivery of goods and services that make life better. Ergo, an attack on business is an attack on quality of life.

And any attack on the financial markets is an attack on business. I suppose one could make a list of businesses that, from cradle to adulthood, have been entirely self-funded. It will not be a very long list. Most businesses require capital to start, and most businesses do not generate cash until after they have started. American financial markets, without any provocation or encouragement from government, organically developed an entire industry known as "venture capital" over the last four decades. It has provided capital to countless technology start-ups that have changed the world. The financial terms were set by private economic actors and administered by risk-taking entrepreneurs and investors, and the sophisticated models in which such firms and investors interacted with developers, programmers, and proprietors were all the work of the invisible hand of American financial markets.

The glory of venture capital in creating Google and Facebook can obscure the countless ways in which American financial markets have improved life outside of Silicon Valley and Wall Street. Small businesses seek debt- and equity-capital partners every day, whether to start up or to expand. Financial markets are the best way to price the risk accurately. Heavy collateral, significant streams of cash flow, and strong inventories tend to provide capital access at a lower cost; more-speculative, open-ended, less collateralized ventures tend to require greater cost of capital (in the form of equity). The existence of liquid, sophisticated financial markets—from conventional debt, to various categories of equity, to complex structures that perhaps combine features of the two—is part of the majesty of the American economy. Put differently, we do not have binary markets—one for high risk and one for low or no risk. The depth, complexity, and nuance of our free-enterprise system, along with advanced capital markets, has created a multitude of options for investors, borrowers, creditors, and every category of financial actor to access capital markets.

Efficient pricing of risk benefits not just investors and entrepreneurs but customers as well. Think of the downward pressure on borrowing costs that greater choice has brought to the debt markets. Relaxed debt-service obligations create greater profits for investors, lower prices for customers, or, as is actually the case, both.

A more sophisticated intellectual framework for finance, combined with the continuation of the Hamiltonian tradition in fervently seeking more evolved capital markets, has also created a division of labor that we all intuitively know works in every other business and sector. Company ABC now has the ability to shop for one set of terms in real-estate lending and another for its equipment-leasing needs. It can then turn to a different financial institution for its depository needs, and a different company still to ask for advice on mergers and acquisitions. At each link in the supply chain of financial advice, the development of sophisticated capital markets has fostered greater talent and placed it in more specialized silos. The benefits to the company, its employees, and its investors are hard to appreciate fully, as is the resulting competitiveness that has made American capital markets the envy of the world.

The common objection to all this is that the echelons of finance are no longer filled with those generating capital for business development or expansion, but rather those just pushing paper back and forth, resulting in no direct benefit to the entrepreneurs whose businesses are represented in the debt and equity securities. But this straw man is not taken seriously by anyone actually in the field of finance who can see the benefits of capital markets. It is prima facie true that hedge funds trading bond paper with another, and technological advances in high-frequency trading, appear to be adding no value to the economy. And yet no critic bemoaning the allegedly vast amounts of worthless economic activity has been able to explain why bid–ask spreads (the difference between what a buyer pays and what a seller gets) have fallen to the lowest level since they began to be measured. Prices of stocks and bonds—when purchased by mutual funds, exchange-traded funds, small investors, retirees, pension funds, and the whole gamut of regular people—include lower transaction costs, and are set in more-liquid markets, than ever before. If this is vulture capitalism, I'll have more, please.

Lack of nuance and inability to make distinctions between key financial actors and roles are not mere ignorance. Hedge funds (asset managers trading their own capital, and often that of other highly accredited investors), private equity (an innovation in capital markets over the last 30 years that has revolutionized company access to capital for growth and strategic expansion), and investment banks (financial institutions providing advice on company strategy and structure, and, in many cases, access to capital markets) are distinct enough, and provide different enough services in financial markets, that the only purpose in blending them all together into some sinister Gordon Gekko caricature is to poison the well and relieve oneself of the burden of making or rebutting a specific argument.

American capital markets are the envy of the world, and rightfully so. Most important, sophisticated avenues of finance have served producers, consumers, job creators, job seekers, and investors for decades. Bad actors exist in financial services, just as bad actors exist in technology, consumer goods, and telecommunications. But to oppose capital markets is to argue for undermining the survival of our free-enterprise system. And perhaps critics of finance know that better than we think?

# CAPITALISM IN AMERICA

## An immigrant perspective

### BY HELEN RALEIGH

RECENTLY I decided to give our kitchen a facelift by adding a fresh coat of paint. Nothing fancy, just some clean and crisp white. I ended up spending more than an hour at Sherwin-Williams because there are several dozen off-white color schemes to choose from. The young clerk joked that it would be nice if we lived in a world with limited choices. I reminded him that there is nothing nice about living in such a world. I know because I have firsthand experience.

I was born and raised in Communist China. If I have to pick one word to describe my childhood, that word is "scarcity." Every essential, from rice to coal, was distributed to each household based on an elaborate government-run ration system. It seemed the more the government dictated, the worse the shortage became.

I still remember the experience of buying our family's first refrigerator in the late '80s. We had to stand in a long line until it was our turn. For the domestic brand we could afford, there was only one size and color available in the store. If we said no, 100 other people would be more than happy to take our fridge home. So we agreed to pick the first one we saw. After it was delivered to our home, my parents proudly put it in the most visible place in the living room and my mom even made a jacket for it to "protect" it from dust.

But limited material choices weren't the worst part of this life. For my parents' generation, upon graduation from college, the government decided where each student would live and for whom he or she would work. So both of my parents ended up living in a small town that is almost a thousand miles away from their schools and hometowns. Worrying about losing food rations forced many young people to accept any form of employment, anywhere the government assigned them. After witnessing how little control my parents had over their lives, I was determined not to live like that.

With the help of a visiting American professor, I became a graduate student in an American college. I arrived in America in 1996 with less than $100 in my pocket. As was true for millions with a craving for freedom who came before me, my pocket was light but my dreams were rich. I took three part-time jobs, including washing mountains of dishes and scrubbing toilets at Chinese restaurants while working on my first master's degree. Life was hard, yet I was blissful. For the very first time in my life, I had the freedom to define my future as I saw fit. I was the sole person responsible for my happiness.

Over the years I worked for several financial-services firms—which clued me in to a business opportunity. After the financial crisis, many people began looking for alternatives to the big financial-services companies they had lost confidence in. In addition, American women are increasingly creating more wealth for themselves and their families—it's estimated that within a decade, more than 65 percent of all private wealth in the U.S. will be held by women—and yet more than two-thirds of American women do not have a financial adviser, partly because of the fact that traditional financial-services firms have done a poor job serving women. In response, I founded Red Meadow Advisors, a fee-only, independent investment-advisory firm focused on helping women achieve financial freedom.

At the time I started my business, I had zero assets under management and zero clients. My sister-in-law, probably out of sympathy, became my first. I framed a copy of the first check she paid me. Today I manage a multi-million-dollar investment portfolio for more than two dozen clients. Most of my clients are women (I do have a few male clients). I am honored to help these productive Americans preserve and grow their hard-earned wealth.

I wouldn't be where I am today without the market economy. Compared with a centrally planned, command-and-control economic model, the market economy is much superior in at least three ways, all of which are readily apparent in my own line of work.

First, healthy competition improves the quality of services while lowering the cost. In the past, only the rich could afford professional investment advisers; the average trading commission was $45 in the 1980s. Today investors pay as little as $7 per trade, the popularity of low-cost index funds has driven down the management fees of many actively managed funds, and the introduction of "robot advisers" has forced many human advisers to cut fees.

Second, contrary to its critics, the free-market economy isn't only about competition; it enhances cooperation, too. Investing is a complex business. Many actions are required, including analyzing, pricing, trading, matching buyers and sellers, moving money and securities to the right accounts, and meeting compliance requirements. The reason that an individual can run an investment company is that thousands of firms, big and small, offer products and services that make what we do possible.

Third, a market economy is the best guarantor of freedom. Each one of us is free to choose how to live, whom to work for, whom we want to work with, and what to buy and sell.

Had I stayed in China, it would have been impossible for me to start my investment business. The Chinese government directs seemingly unlimited resources to state-run companies and a few government-selected "private" businesses (a.k.a. "national champions"); aspiring entrepreneurs have no chance to compete. Further, the *Wall Street Journal* reports that the Chinese government uses surveillance tools to monitor traders, including "warning brokerage firms to police trades that are out of step with government wishes and phoning investors directly when they act out of line."

Fortunately, I get to choose to do what I love because I live in a free country with a vibrant market economy. It's sad to see a growing number of Americans today either express serious doubts about markets or reject them outright.

# THE MARKET TRADITION

## Capitalism draws on pre-liberal roots that are important today

**BY YUVAL LEVIN**

We live in an era of collapsing confidence in institutions, and the market economy has been no exception. Polls show declining support for capitalism, especially among the young. And the market system is increasingly under attack not only from the left but from some smart social conservatives, populists, and nationalists on the right. To effectively defend democratic capitalism, its champions will need to understand the nature of these criticisms, to see where they have a point, and to think about how to make a case for markets that takes them seriously.

Not all the contemporary critics of capitalism are all that serious, of course, just as not all its defenders are. But those who voice the deepest grievances have in common some complaints that should not be ignored.

For the most part, these complaints are not fundamentally economic but rather are moral. This sometimes is not obvious even to the people lodging them. But arguments about inequalities of wealth or power, cronyism and special-interest influence, a shallow consumerism that corrupts the soul and undermines the dignity of work, a stateless cosmopolitanism that neglects national priorities, and a commitment to creative destruction over protective preservation are arguments about the ends of capitalism at least as much as its means. They accuse our society of a failure to prioritize the highest things, and so they charge us with moral failings embodied in a corrupt political economy.

This means, for one thing, that evidence of capitalism's ability to produce prosperity will be of limited use in response. It is important to make people aware that the market system has brought billions out of grinding poverty and continues to do so still. This is essential to the moral case for capitalism and is an answer to the shallowest charges against it. But if the market were in fact, as some of its critics suggest, a great machine for replacing material poverty with moral poverty, then evidence of its success in reducing deprivation would not be proof against the charge that it produces depravity. Similarly, evidence of economic growth is not an answer to the charge that overall prosperity comes at costs to some particular Americans that should be unacceptable to all of us.

The case for markets as engines of liberty is crucial to the defense of capitalism too, but in a similarly constrained way. The right to property is especially vital to human dignity, and no society could be just while violating it or trampling our other liberties. But modern capitalism may not be the only way to respect these rights and liberties, so evidence of the various ways that markets promote and undermine the dignity of persons would have to influence our judgments about when to defend markets and when to criticize them.

The deepest challenges to capitalism therefore have to be answered on the grounds of morality. If, as Irving Kristol once asserted, the market economy promises us wealth, freedom, and a just society, it is the third of these promises that the system's most serious critics insist it is failing to keep. And a sense that our way of life is in some key respects unjust is behind much of our broader loss of faith in institutions too.

Part of a moral defense of the market system would have to shed light on its moral goals and premises. These are not hard to discern, for instance, in the thought of capitalism's intellectual progenitors. Adam Smith was a professor of moral philosophy, and his project sought to ground a modern successor to Aristotelian ethics in a sophisticated sense of human sympathy and sociability. In a free society, Smith suggested, men and women cannot be compelled to act morally, so we require institutions that form our characters and dispositions so that we might *choose* to act morally. The market is one such institution. Through the division of labor, it enables essentially every person to approach the larger society on the basis of what he can offer rather than just what he needs, reinforcing his dignity. And by valuing reliability, honesty, civility, discipline, and similar bourgeois virtues, markets give us the habits required to handle an enormous amount of freedom responsibly. Because they prioritize the needs of consumers, rather than just those of the owners of capital, markets are also powerfully democratizing forces. And because they are so very good at making us productive and rich, they help the poor to rise as well.

That markets can be perverted by cronyism, corruption, self-dealing, and the capture of regulators is not an argument against them. Every system can be so perverted—decidedly including all the modern alternatives to capitalism that the human race has tried. Societies with market economies should do what they can to minimize such corruption and to avoid the circumstances that invite it, but that is more an argument against Medicare for All than a case against capitalism.

And yet, these virtues of the market system alone do not suffice as an answer. Capitalism is most vulnerable to moral critiques because it rests upon a moral foundation that it can also undermine. It requires—for its workers, employers, owners, and investors—a kind of human being that it does not by itself produce and can easily corrupt. Left to itself, it would tend to prioritize consumption over every other human endeavor and profit over every other standard of the good, and so could badly distort our priorities. If our politics and culture were merely extensions of the market system—if market signals were our primary measures of merit, virtue, decency, freedom, responsibility, and worth—then ours would indeed be an unjust society.

But our politics and culture are much more than that. The best case for capitalism is a case for markets as one crucial set of institutions in a free society deeply rooted in the West's liberal and pre-liberal soil. It is crucial because at its best it protects every man's right to the fruits of his labor, encourages virtues crucial to living free, and has proven unbeatably capable of improving everyone's living standards. But it must remain rooted, because man does not live by bread alone, and because both the market and the larger society depend upon other formative institutions that help us all become better human beings and citizens.

These other institutions—the family, religion, schools, civic associations, political bodies, and more—teach and habituate us in ways that encourage distinct virtues of their own. They all have their excesses, to be sure. But they also often work to keep one another in check. Their tensions with the ethos of the market do the same. Communal and national loyalties can make for inefficient economics, and obligations to tithe or observe the Sabbath aren't always great for business. But commitments such as these can help us see that our communities aren't just random collections of labor and capital, our nation isn't just another place to work or invest in, raising children isn't one consumer preference among many, and business isn't everything.

Critics of the market should be willing to acknowledge that it is made better by these countervailing yet supportive institutions throughout our society. But defenders of the market therefore have to make themselves defenders of these other institutions too, and of the social order of which they are all part. The market can advance the cause not only of prosperity but of justice only if it is embedded in this larger whole.

Seeing the virtues of markets in their embeddedness in our larger social order can also help avoid the kinds of utopian arguments for markets that some of their more libertarian defenders sometimes make. The case for markets is a case for humility before the immense complexity of social life.

It begins from our ignorance, and properly understood it should steer us away from overconfidence.

The tensions that arise among the demands of these different institutions and the commitments that constitute our social order can often be addressed by individuals setting priorities in their own lives. But there are also instances when dealing with such tensions requires politics. This means that sometimes our economic policy has to be determined by more than purely economic considerations—by our sense of the kind of society we want to be and the kinds of goals we want to pursue together. Overall economic growth is one such vital goal, as surely everyone agrees. But there are other goals that matter, including equity, cultural vitality, social order, family formation, piety and religious liberty, individual and national self-sufficiency, personal liberty and communal self-determination, and moral traditionalism and moral pluralism, among many others. Ordering these frequently competing or contradictory ends in hard cases is part of what our politics is for, and the argument for capitalism cannot be an argument for putting economics above all else.

To suggest that our commitments to market ideals must be moderated in this way, and also that they should be allowed to moderate some of our other commitments, is not to attack capitalism but to defend it. It is to grasp its full significance, its place in the larger scheme of our free society. Indeed, the same is true of liberalism itself: To show how its strengths can invigorate us while its weaknesses must be mitigated by our other fidelities is to show how liberalism can succeed, not why liberalism failed.

Against its most serious and able critics, then, the market needs defenders who see it as one among the several crucial institutions most indigenous to liberalism, and who acknowledge that, like all the others, it draws on our society's deep roots in pre-liberal traditions and can thrive only as long as it does not twist or sever those. In other words, capitalism needs conservative defenders, and deserves to have them.

# ABOUT *NATIONAL REVIEW*

N*ATIONAL* *REVIEW* is America's premier conservative magazine. Edited by Rich Lowry, the fortnightly was founded in 1955 by William F. Buckley Jr. In its premier issue, the editors stated in the magazine's "Credenda" that among its primary convictions and intentions were the protection of free markets ("the competitive price system is indispensable to liberty and material progress"), the defeat of Socialism ("the century's most blatant force of satanic utopianism"), and the defense of the organic moral order ("the profound crisis of our era"). Famously stating that *National Review* "stands athwart history, yelling Stop," that pledge and commitment—and those philosophical concerns—remain as real and vital today as they were over six decades ago.

Made in the USA
Monee, IL
12 May 2020

30795074R00109